319440

Sue Lawrence's

SCOTTISH
Kitchen

Sue Lawrence's
SCOTTISH Kitchen

headline

For my sister Carol, with love

Also by Sue Lawrence

Scots Cooking
Entertaining at Home in Scotland
Cooking for Pleasure
Food with Flair
Feasting on Herbs
On Baking
The Sunday Times Cookbook

headline

Copyright © 2002 Sue Lawrence

The right of Sue Lawrence to be identified as the Author of
the Work has been asserted by her in accordance with the
Copyright, Designs and Patents Act 1988.

First published in 2002 by
HEADLINE BOOK PUBLISHING

10 9 8 7 6 5 4 3 2 1

British Library Cataloguing in Publication Data

Lawrence, Sue
Sue Lawrence's Scottish kitchen
1.Cookery, Scottish
I.Title II.Scottish kitchen
641.5'9411

ISBN 0 7553 1050 0

Printed and bound in Italy by Poligrafico Dehoniano
Colour reproduction by Spectrum Colour, Ipswich
Designed by Isobel Gillan
Photography by Justin Scobie
Food styling by Maxine Clarke

Headline Book Publishing
A division of Hodder Headline
338 Euston Road
London NW1 3BH

www.headline.co.uk
www.hodderheadline.com

Contents

Introduction

MY SCOTTISH KITCHEN is just like many others. There are the usual pots and pans, whisks and spatulas as well as those gadgets such as food processors and blenders we cannot live without. There is also a porridge spurtle, potato masher and a good array of tart tins and baking sheets – one baking tin being specifically for the weekly batch of shortbread. And, of course, there is the huge brass jam pan ('jeelie pan') on top of the cupboard, with the jelly bag hanging alongside.

And as for ingredients, again my kitchen is similar to many Scottish kitchens. There are, of course, the basics, those ubiquitous must-haves every kitchen from Land's End to Lerwick now carries: from olive oil and best cooking chocolate to dried pasta and jars of pesto. But look carefully in the Scottish kitchen these days and you might see beside the huge box of panettone (you know, the one you were given last Christmas) a splendid Selkirk bannock. Beside the Brie or Stilton, there might be a Scottish Carola or Lanark Blue. Instead of bundles of pak choi or piles of purslane, there could be a whole turnip (swede) or bag of kale, straight from the local organic box. Beside the couscous, a packet of barley from the north of Scotland, and beside the polenta, three different cuts of oatmeal. There is marmalade – and jam made from Scottish strawberries or raspberries – and in the bread bin beside the granary loaf are some oatcakes and barley bannocks.

As for raw ingredients, the list is endless: from humble Ayrshire bacon, black pudding and Arbroath smokies to some of the finest game, beef and lamb you will find anywhere in the world; the choice is vast. And, thankfully, having taken a good look round the rest of the world for culinary inspiration over the past few decades, we have at last returned to our roots and realised that since Scottish produce is sublime, why not use it – but use it simply, for that is what we do best. And although we do not necessarily want to be for ever preparing the traditional dishes that often require long, slow cooking, we can adapt to the present day and use modern, funkier recipes in our own kitchen, whilst showcasing that wonderful produce at the same time.

And so in this book – a celebration of Scottish produce in the modern kitchen – you will find such dishes as *Lobster, chips and mayo*, *Langoustine mash*, *Steak pie with olives*, *Tayberry and blackcurrant slump* or *Parmesan shortbread*. Some are adaptations of the old favourites, some are new dishes invented around specific produce: for example *Smoked haddock brandade* or *Slow-cooked lamb with chermoula*. All use typically Scottish ingredients; all are, to my mind, utterly delicious. But then, I would say that – it is my Scottish kitchen. And, as I said earlier, my own kitchen is just like many others. In fact, it is just like yours.

Sue Lawrence

Hearty breakfasts

SOME OF THE FOOD on offer at breakfast these days is grim. From garishly coloured and sugar-laden cereals to gristly sausages made with minimal meat, Day-Glo-yellow smoked haddock and – one of the worst – pop tarts. And I refer to the latter not in my sanctimonious 'work of the devil' puritan mode, but as a mother who has had to deprive her youngest from her longing to eat these at breakfast, having had them at a friend's house and found them divine. In food, as in life, there is no accounting for taste.

In Scotland, we have always been rather good at breakfasts. Remember Samuel Johnson's singular comment on our food in 1773 (one of the few written in an approving and complimentary manner): 'If an epicure could remove by a wish, in quest of sensual gratifications, wherever he had supped he would breakfast in Scotland.'

Alas, much has changed and people grab whatever they can as they rush around looking for lost socks or car keys. There are, however, shining beacons of matutinal culinary excellence, the sort of place that makes you want morning to go on for ever. Whether in a smart hotel or humble bed and breakfast, to sit down to a leisurely breakfast of porridge, poached eggs, black pudding and mushrooms (I know, not a regular combination, but all of which I adore), served with plenty of thick granary toast and endless pots of tea, is my idea of bliss. At one of my favourite Scottish hotels, Turnberry Hotel in Ayrshire, the porridge is so good it is almost worth getting up really early to have a bracing walk along the sea-shore, which is directly over the road from the dining room, in order to allow yourself two bowls. Made purely with pinhead oatmeal, this is the real thing, soaked overnight then lovingly stirred for up to an hour until thick, creamy and utterly divine.

And whether you opt for a cereal-based start to your day or some tasty dish made with eggs, smoked fish or even venison kidneys, I think it is imperative to eat something, not only to kick-start the brain but also to deal with early morning grumpiness which can only be eliminated by eating something. But preferably not a pop tart.

Porridge was my staple breakfast as a child, come rain or shine. And it was often served with stewed rhubarb or apples – a cursory nod towards healthy fruit consumption, I suppose. We Scots have not exactly been known for our addiction to fresh fruit.

Although it is anathema to those old-fashioned porridge eaters who ate it in the classic way – flavoured only with salt, never sugar, and served in one bowl with spoonfuls dipped into a smaller bowl of cold milk – I suggest you serve the rhubarb on top and then drizzle over some single cream or top of the milk. Absolutely divine; just don't tell the salt-only purists.

I normally use coarse oatmeal, but half medium, half pinhead gives a lovely texture.

Porridge with stewed rhubarb

SERVES 4

1 large cup (or mug) of oatmeal
700g/1 lb 9 oz young rhubarb, trimmed and chopped into 2cm/³/₄ inch pieces
50g/1³/₄ oz golden caster sugar
1 teaspoon vanilla extract
a pinch of salt

The night before, place the oatmeal in a saucepan with 3 large cups (or mugs) of cold water. Leave to soak overnight.

For the rhubarb, which can also be cooked the day before, place the prepared rhubarb, sugar and vanilla in a saucepan with 3 tablespoons of water and bring very slowly to the boil. Cook, uncovered, for 3–5 minutes or until the rhubarb is just tender. Remove from the heat, cover and leave to cool.

For the porridge, add the salt to the oatmeal in the pan and bring slowly to the boil. In Scottish kitchens, porridge is traditionally stirred with a long wooden stick called a spurtle (or theevil). So, stirring often, cook for about 10–15 minutes, or until thick and creamy. Serve in warm bowls with some rhubarb spooned on top and a good splash of milk or cream.

Whenever I am in the United States, I love having breakfast in a diner, and if home-made granola is on the menu, I opt for this first, with perhaps a smattering of blueberries on top.

Oat granola with brazil nuts and apricots

MAKES about 1kg/2¼ lb

200g/7 oz brazil nuts
½ teaspoon ground cinnamon
500g/1 lb 2 oz jumbo oatflakes
100g/3½ oz desiccated coconut
250g/9 oz unsalted butter
225g/8 oz runny honey
150g/5½ oz dried apricots,
  chopped
50g/1¾ oz raisins

Preheat the oven to 170°C/325°F/Gas 3.

Place the brazil nuts in a food processor with the cinnamon. Add a handful of the oatflakes and then process very briefly (I use the pulse button) – only for about 10 seconds – until the nuts are chopped into good-sized chunks. Do not over-process; you want roughly chopped nuts, not a paste. Tip them into a bowl with the remaining oatflakes and the coconut, stirring well.

Melt the butter and honey together in a pan; then stir into the oat mixture until combined thoroughly.

Lightly grease two 23 × 33cm/9 × 13 in Swiss-roll tins with butter then divide the granola mixture between the tins and pat down evenly.

Place the tins in the preheated oven for about 30 minutes or until golden brown. (If you have both tins in one oven, the lower tray may need longer to crisp.)

Allow the granola to cool completely; once cold, it will be solid enough to break into large pieces. Place these, together with all the smaller pieces and crumbs, in a bowl and break up roughly. Finally, stir in the dried fruit.

Stored in an airtight container, the granola will keep for a few weeks.

It is essential to use authentic Greek yoghurt for this – not 'Greek-style' yoghurt since that is not thick and creamy enough. And use only light muscovado sugar: after a good chilling, the sugar sprinkled on top of the yoghurt transforms miraculously into a gooey, fudgy layer.

This will certainly perk up your morning … depending on how much whisky you use to anoint the oranges.

Whisky oranges with fudgy Greek yoghurt

SERVES 3–4

250ml/9 fl oz Greek yoghurt
2 tablespoons light muscovado sugar
2 large oranges
whisky (preferably malt)

Tip the yoghurt into a shallow serving dish and level out the surface. Sprinkle over the sugar, trying to cover the yoghurt completely. Place, uncovered, in the fridge for at least 12 hours.

Carefully peel the oranges, being sure to remove all the pith, and thinly slice, discarding the pips. It is a good idea to do this over the dish in which you are going to serve the oranges so that the juice is collected.

Place the orange slices in the dish with all the juices. Drizzle over some whisky (the amount depends on personal preference – and who will be eating the orange slices). If possible, chill for an hour or so.

Serve the orange slices with a large spoonful of fudgy yoghurt.

These banana- and bramble-flavoured, crunchy oat-topped muffins are a doddle to prepare and take only 20 minutes to bake. So this is a recipe you can rustle up as your family or guests are still slumbering. I assure you, the homely baking aromas will soon lure them downstairs.

Banana and bramble oaty muffins

MAKES 12 American-size muffins

150g/5½ oz butter, melted and
   cooled slightly
55g/2 oz golden caster sugar
2 large free-range eggs, beaten
200ml/7 fl oz milk
grated zest and juice of
   ½ unwaxed lemon
2 small ripe bananas, mashed
250g/9 oz self-raising flour, sifted
250g /9 oz brambles
   (blackberries)
40g /1½ oz jumbo oatflakes
40g /1½ oz light muscovado
   sugar

Preheat the oven to 200°C/400°F/Gas 6.

   Place the first 5 ingredients in a bowl and stir to combine. Stir in the bananas, and then fold in the flour with a gentle action. Tip in the brambles and very lightly stir to combine: do not beat madly or they will bleed purple into the mixture.

   Place 12 large paper muffin cases in a bun tin and then spoon in the mixture.

   Combine the oatflakes and the muscovado sugar and sprinkle some over the top of each muffin case.

   Bake in the preheated oven for about 20 minutes, or until golden brown and cooked through. The muffins are best eaten straightaway when they are warm, but they will reheat if necessary.

For a truly special morning treat, make this for breakfast or brunch. You can add more or less smoked salmon depending on how much you can afford, but do not add any more chervil since its delicate aniseed flavour should not overpower the eggs. Smoked salmon pieces are fine and are also cheaper.

Cold smoked trout is also good for this dish – or fresh crab meat. And instead of chervil, you could add dill or snipped chives for a change.

Serve on thick wholemeal toast or toasted bagels. If you make it with crab instead of salmon, it is delicious served on toasted brioche.

Scrambled eggs with smoked salmon

SERVES 2

6 medium free-range eggs

2 tablespoons single cream or top of the milk

salt and freshly ground black pepper

40g /1¹/₂ oz butter

about 50g/1³/₄ oz smoked salmon, chopped roughly

1 heaped tablespoon freshly chopped chervil

Lightly beat together the eggs and cream or top of the milk and season with plenty of salt and pepper.

Slowly melt the butter in a saucepan (or small frying pan) over a low heat, and then add the egg mixture. Stirring constantly, cook over a low heat until still creamy and soft (up to 5 minutes, depending on your pan).

Remove from the heat to arrest the cooking and stir in the salmon and most of the chervil. Taste and check the seasoning. Serve in a pile on hot toast. Sprinkle with the remaining chervil and serve at once.

Although hot-smoked trout would also do for this delicious breakfast dish, cold-smoked trout (which resembles smoked salmon) is my favourite. As it is added shortly before serving, it only heats through and does not cook and therefore retains its distinctive flavour.

Instead of parsnips, you could use all potatoes if you prefer.

Smoked trout hash

SERVES 6

500g/1 lb 2 oz large potatoes, peeled

250g/9 oz parsnips, peeled

salt and freshly ground black pepper

2 tablespoons olive oil

25g/1 oz butter

1 large onion, peeled and sliced

250–300g/9–10½ oz cold-smoked trout, roughly chopped

2 tablespoons freshly chopped dill or parsley

Cook the potatoes and parsnips whole in boiling salted water until just tender (about 15 minutes). Drain well, allow to cool a little, then cut into large dice.

In a large, heavy frying pan, heat the oil and butter, and then fry the onion for 5 minutes until soft. Add the potatoes and parsnips and fry over a medium heat for 10–12 minutes, stirring occasionally, until the mixture forms crusted, golden edges. Season well with salt and pepper.

Stir in the smoked trout and dill or parsley and continue to cook for a further 4–5 minutes or until heated through. Check the seasoning and serve hot.

Tattie scones are nothing like regular scones which are tall, light and airy (in theory!). These are girdle scones, not unlike soda scones or farls. They are wonderful for breakfast with bacon or a good slice of grilled black pudding – but they are also delicious spread with butter and jam for tea.

The best varieties of potato to use are Golden Wonder, Maris Piper or Pentland Dell.

Tattie scones with bacon

SERVES 4

250g/9 oz floury potatoes, peeled
25g/1 oz butter and extra for
   greasing girdle
50g/1¾ oz plain flour
½ teaspoon salt
¼ teaspoon baking powder
8 rashers of back or middle bacon,
   preferably Ayrshire bacon

Cut the potatoes into chunks; then cook in boiling water until tender. Drain thoroughly until completely dry and then mash with the butter. Weigh it out: you should have about 200g/7 oz warm, mashed potato.

Sift the flour, salt and baking powder into a bowl. Stir in the still warm mash and combine well, but gently, to make a dough.

Using lightly floured hands, gently shape the dough into 2 balls and turn on to a lightly floured surface. Roll out gently with a rolling pin to form 2 circles, 5mm/¼ in thick. Cut each circle into quarters and prick all over with a fork.

Heat a girdle (griddle) or large, heavy frying pan to medium-hot then smear over a little butter. Once hot, carefully transfer 4 scones (I use a large spatula) and cook for about 3–4 minutes on each side, until golden brown. Transfer the scones to a wire rack while you cook the second batch.

Grill the bacon until crisp. To serve, place 2 scones on each plate and top with bacon.

These make an excellent – and substantial – breakfast dish.
Although haddock is the main fish used in Scotland, cod or
perhaps coley would also work very well. The best varieties of
potato to use are Charlotte, Estima or Belle de Fontenay.

If you are having the fish cakes for brunch, you might think
about serving them with an anchovy-spiked mayonnaise; for
breakfast, just serve au naturel.

Rosti fish cakes

SERVES 4–5

500g/1 lb 2 oz waxy potatoes
500g/1 lb 2 oz haddock fillets,
cut into large chunks
1 tablespoon freshly chopped
chives
1 medium free-range egg
salt and freshly ground black
pepper
2 tablespoons sunflower oil

Peel and coarsely grate the potatoes and pat dry with kitchen paper.
Place the fish, chives, egg, salt and pepper in a food processor and, using the pulse button, process briefly until combined: do not over-process or you will have a gluey paste. Mix this with the potatoes, then divide into 9–10 balls and flatten out slightly.
Line a plate with kitchen paper and place the fish cakes on it. Chill for 1 hour or so, then pat dry again.
Preheat the oven to 150°C/300°F/Gas 2.
Heat the oil in a frying pan and, once very hot, brown the fish cakes for 3–4 minutes, then turn and brown the other side. Place them on a baking sheet and cook in the preheated oven for about 30 minutes or until the cakes are piping hot and cooked through. Serve warm.

When I bumped into my friend Clarissa Dickson Wright at Edinburgh's Farmers' Market one day last summer (bitingly cold wind, double thermals), she insisted on introducing me to the world of venison kidneys at a new stall which sold wild venison. Having never tried them before, I was game. (Sorry…)

Although the kidneys I tried were from red deer and are the easiest to obtain, according to Clarissa an even finer treat is from roe deer, so do look out for them. After a breakfast of these delicious kidneys, all will be well with your day ahead, I can assure you.

Be nice to your butcher, and he will skin and core the kidneys for you.

Venison kidneys on toast

**ENOUGH FOR 1 hearty breakfast
  (or for 2 as part of a regular fry-up)**

**1 venison kidney (a red deer's will
  weigh about 175g/6 oz),
  skinned and cored**
butter
**salt and freshly ground black
  pepper**
2 thick slices wholemeal bread

Split the kidney in half lengthways, and pat dry. Heat a good knob of butter in a pan and, once sizzling, add the 2 kidney halves. Season with salt and pepper. After 1 minute, turn down the heat and turn the kidneys over. Now cook gently until just done: the kidneys should still be slightly pink in the middle. I reckon no longer than 3–4 minutes in total is needed; overcook them and they will be rubbery.

Meanwhile, toast the bread and butter it. Place the kidneys on the toast with any pan juices poured over.

I absolutely adore black pudding, but only the best will do. I am sorry to say I dislike many French boudins and Sassenach puddings with their knobbly bits of fat studded throughout, and prefer the Scottish variety that has finely shredded fat all the way through. I also love the flavour of many Scottish black puddings – particularly the Stornoway pudding produced by Charlie Barley, the brilliant butcher in Stornoway on the Isle of Lewis, which are made with sheep's blood instead of pig's or ox blood. And it is also primarily oatmeal that is used as the cereal thickener.

Black pudding with pan-fried apples

During the millennium celebrations, we had a brunch for some sixty friends and family, and served Bloody Marys and porridge, and then bacon and black pudding rolls. Both bacon (Ayrshire middle) and pudding were barbecued outside (yes, in Scotland, in January) and served in a soft, floury bap, the black pudding ones with just a slice of tomato between the roll and the crisply barbecued pudding. Having ordered eight dozen rolls from Joe at the corner shop, he could hardly believe it when, a couple of hours into brunch, one of the children was dispatched for another two dozen rolls. He therefore did not seem surprised when another child (just over the legal age to buy alcohol) was sent round soon after for two extra bottles of vodka for even more Bloody Marys. The party, if I recall correctly, went on well into the afternoon, and then evening. Black pudding and Bloody Marys are obviously a winning combination: try it with this delicious recipe.

SERVES 4

2 tablespoons olive oil

8 slices black pudding

25g/1 oz butter

2 large Cox or Egremont Russet apples, peeled and thickly sliced

Heat the oil in a frying pan until very hot, then fry the black pudding until it is crispy outside and soft inside which will take 3–5 minutes, turning once. Meanwhile, heat the butter in another frying pan, quickly fry the apple slices for 3–4 minutes until they are tinged golden brown.

Place the black pudding on 4 warm plates, then top with the apple slices.

A fly cup

WHEN I WAS A CHILD, home-baking was part of everyone's diet. Even though there might not have been three-tiered iced cakes every day, there was always something when you came in from school, whether it was a simple pancake, warm from the girdle, or a treacle scone, dripping with butter. It was quite simply a part of life.

There is, of course, different terminology throughout Scotland, but 'teabreads' is generally recognised as the word for all manner of cakes, scones and cookies eaten with a cup of tea. And tea (afternoon tea, not high tea which is a meal in itself) was often referred to – especially in Aberdeenshire – as a 'fly cup' or even a 'fly cuppie'. With this would come a 'fine piece' – something tasty, usually sweet, invariably home-baked. Fancy cakes were called 'puffie-toots' (or tooties) in Angus and there are other wonderful words in the Scots dialect such as a 'cookie shine' meaning a tea party.

Other specifically Scots words are still used for certain types of cake or biscuit. When I visited Alan McPherson, the baker in Cullen on the north Aberdeenshire coast, to watch him make butteries through the night, I was also impressed by his 'sair heidies' – small, plain sponge cakes with a paper band round the lower part and topped with pink icing and a blood-red glacé cherry, all symbolising a sore head swaddled in bleeding bandages. 'Heckle biscuits' (or hecklies), which are similar to raggie biscuits, are buttery, short biscuits still found in Fife and Dundee. 'Halie dabbies' are a kind of shortbread formerly used instead of bread at communion. And 'puggy buns' – a spiced gingerbread-type filling (called gundy) encased in short pastry – are a speciality of Fife and are still made by baker Kenny Adamson in Pittenweem.

With such a gloriously rich language, is it little wonder that we are justifiably proud of our baking in the Scottish kitchen? The recipes in this chapter – from *Chocolate brownies with raspberries*, *Blackcurrant crumble cake* and *Marmalade and oatmeal gingerbread* to *Parmesan shortbread* (sacrilege to shortbread purists!) – might not sound quite as evocative as those traditional Scots ones, but I can assure you they taste utterly delicious. Go on; try some with your fly cup.

These lovely crisp little savoury biscuits are excellent served with pre-prandial drinks; they can accompany anything from a Pimm's or a gin and tonic to a sophisticated glass of champagne. They are also good served with a bowl of hearty winter soup – or, of course, a cup of afternoon tea.

Parmesan shortbread

MAKES 18–20

75g/2¾ oz freshly grated Parmesan

75g/2¾ oz unsalted butter, slightly softened

¼ teaspoon salt

75g/2¾ oz plain flour, sifted

Place all the ingredients in a food processor and process briefly – just until they are combined and are forming large clumps.

Take the mixture from the food processor in your hands and place it on a sheet of clingfilm. Roll the mixture into a long sausage shape, about 23cm/9 in long. Chill well for an hour or so (or pop it in the freezer for 20 minutes) until firm. Meanwhile, preheat the oven to 150°C/300°F/Gas 2. Grease a baking sheet with butter

Use a very sharp knife to cut the sausage into 18–20 thin slices. Place these on the prepared baking sheet and prick each with a fork.

Bake them in the preheated oven for 18–20 minutes, or until they are a pale golden brown.

Place the cooked biscuits on a wire rack to cool before serving.

This is a gorgeous, moist, coconut cake with a lemony almond base and light crunchy crust. It is perfect for afternoon tea but also delicious for pudding, served with some seasonal berries and maybe a dollop of clotted cream.

Macaroon cake

SERVES 8

FOR THE BASE
150g/5½ oz ground almonds
100g/3½ oz plain flour, sifted
100g/3½ oz golden caster sugar
150g/5½ oz butter, slightly
    softened
grated zest of 1 unwaxed lemon

FOR THE FILLING
5 large free-range eggs, separated
325g/11½ oz desiccated coconut
40g/1½ oz butter, melted
300g/10½ oz golden caster sugar

Preheat the oven to 170°C/325°F/Gas 3. Grease a 24cm/9½ in springform cake tin with butter.

For the base, place the first three ingredients in a food processor and combine. Then add the butter and lemon zest and process briefly until the mixture looks as if you could bring it together in your hands. Place the mixture in the prepared cake tin and press it well into the base and a little way up the sides.

For the filling, beat together the egg yolks and coconut, then add the melted butter.

Whisk the egg whites until stiff, then gradually beat in the sugar, a spoonful at a time. Beat until glossy. Gently fold this into the egg yolk and coconut mixture. Then spoon the filling into the cake base.

Bake in the preheated oven for about 1 hour or until the cake is lightly golden and just firm to the touch. Cool the cake on a wire rack before decanting it to a serving plate.

This is a wonderfully rich cake that is completely devoid of wheat flour and therefore suitable for coeliacs.

Serve it cold with tea, or very slightly warmed with thick cream for pudding.

No-flour nutty chocolate cake

SERVES 8

250g/9 oz whole blanched
   hazelnuts
250g/9 oz unsalted butter
250g/9 oz dark chocolate
   (60–70% cocoa solids)
6 large free-range eggs, separated
200g/7 oz golden caster sugar
a pinch of salt

Preheat the oven to 170°C/325°F/Gas 3.

Place the nuts on a baking tray and roast in the oven for about 15 minutes or until they darken slightly. You should also be able to detect a faintly nutty aroma. Remove (leaving the oven on) and tip the nuts into a food processor or grinder and grind to a coarse meal.

Melt the butter and chocolate, stir to combine and then allow the mixture to cool slightly. Beat the egg yolks with the sugar until thick. Beat the egg whites until stiff but not too dry.

Fold the egg yolk mixture into the chocolate mixture with the salt, then fold in the ground hazelnuts. Fold in the whites gently, a little at a time.

Grease a 24cm/9½ in springform cake tin with butter and line the base with greaseproof paper. Tip the mixture into the prepared cake tin and bake in the preheated oven for about 40 minutes or until it feels firm when you place your hand lightly on top.

Remove the cake from the oven, let it rest for at least 10 minutes, then remove the sides of the tin and allow the cake to cool completely on a wire rack.

These dark chocolate brownies are all-year-round family staples in my house. Hardly a week goes by without my rustling up a batch. But the combination of chocolate and raspberries is sublime and during the raspberry season, when I add berries to the brownies, they are even more scrumptious. I have tried making them with frozen fruit in winter but the mixture is rather too moist: it still tastes good but is impossible to lift out of the tin.

I go to the West Craigie fruit farm near Edinburgh during the strawberry and raspberry season, but if I am visiting relatives in Dundee, I stop off at one of the fruit farms in the Carse of Gowrie between Dundee and Perth – both this area and further north around Blairgowrie are home to the best raspberries in the world.

Chocolate brownies with raspberries

MAKES 16

**350g/12 oz dark chocolate
(55–60% cocoa solids)**
250g/9 oz unsalted butter
3 large free-range eggs
250g/9 oz dark muscovado sugar
100g/3¹/₂ oz plain flour, sifted
1 teaspoon baking powder
a pinch of salt
175g/6 oz fresh raspberries

Preheat the oven to 170°C/325°F/Gas 3. Butter a 23cm/9 in square cake tin.

Melt the chocolate and butter together, then cool slightly.

Whisk the eggs until thick, then gradually add the sugar and beat until glossy. Beat in the melted chocolate mixture, then gently fold in the flour, baking powder and salt.

Pour just over half the mixture into the prepared cake tin. Scatter over the raspberries, then cover with the remaining mixture.

Bake in the preheated oven for about 40 minutes or until the surface is set. It will be cooked when a skewer inserted into the middle comes out with just a little mixture adhering.

Remove the cake to a wire rack, and allow it to rest for about 20 minutes. Cut the cake into squares and remove them from the tin when cold. (It is seriously tempting to remove them when they are still warm but they are too fragile to decant unless cold.)

This can be served cold with your afternoon cup of tea or warm for pudding with cream or yoghurt. Raspberries are also good in this recipe, but decrease the sugar in the crumble topping by about 40g/1½ oz.

If you want to take this cake with you on a picnic, instead of cutting and removing the squares from the tin once it is baked, you can cool it in the tin, then loosely wrap the tin in foil and cut it in situ.

Blackcurrant crumble cake

MAKES 24 squares

FOR THE BASE
350g/12 oz plain flour, sifted
50g/1¾ oz golden caster sugar
200g/7 oz unsalted butter, diced
a pinch of salt
2 medium free-range eggs, beaten

FOR THE FILLING AND CRUMBLE
75g/2¾ oz plain flour, sifted
75g/2¾ oz porridge oats
150g/5½ oz golden caster sugar
125g/4½ oz unsalted butter, diced
1 rounded teaspoon ground cinnamon
grated zest of 1 unwaxed lemon
2 tablespoons semolina
500g/1 lb 2 oz fresh blackcurrants

Preheat the oven to 200°C/400°F/Gas 6. Butter a 23 × 33cm/ 9 × 13 in Swiss-roll tin.

For the base, place the flour, sugar, butter and salt in a food processor and process briefly until it resembles breadcrumbs. Slowly add the eggs through the feeder tube and process very briefly, until just combined. Press the dough into the prepared tin, smoothing the surface.

For the crumble, place the flour, oats, sugar, butter, cinnamon and lemon zest in a bowl. Rub in the butter until the mixture is crumbly.

Scatter the semolina over the dough in the tin, then carefully tip in the blackcurrants, trying to ensure they are evenly distributed.

Top with the crumble mixture and very gently press down, trying to cover most of the currants. Bake in the preheated oven for 20 minutes, then reduce the temperature to 180°C/350°F/Gas 4 and continue to bake for about another 30 minutes, or until the cake is golden brown.

Leave the cake to cool for about 30 minutes, then cut into squares and remove to a wire rack to cool completely.

This is based on fellow food writer Carol Wilson's recipe for a dark and, most importantly, moist gingerbread; don't you just hate dry gingerbread? I have incorporated a little oatmeal into the mixture, so it is similar to Orkney broonie, an oatmeal-based gingerbread from the Orkney Islands. But instead of using traditional black treacle in the mixture, this one has molasses sugar which does away with the messy weighing out of treacle. There is also marmalade which enhances the rich, dark flavours of the cake.

In and around Dundee, my home town, marmalade is not only used in cakes, it is also often mixed into Cloutie dumpling, that most glorious of Scottish puddings, a treat on birthdays, high days and holidays. And, coincidentally, although Carol now lives in the Wirral, her father is from Tayport, just over the Tay Bridge from Dundee, so marmalade is obviously in the blood.

Marmalade and oatmeal gingerbread

SERVES 10

225g/8 oz butter

225g/8 oz unrefined molasses sugar

300ml/½ pint milk

225g/8 oz marmalade

325g/11½ oz plain flour, sifted

40g/1½ oz medium oatmeal

1 tablespoon ground ginger

¼ teaspoon ground nutmeg

2 teaspoons bicarbonate of soda

2 medium free-range eggs, beaten

4–5 balls of stem ginger,
   chopped finely

100g/3½ oz sultanas or raisins

Preheat the oven to 150°C/300°F/Gas 2. Butter a 23cm/9 in square cake tin and line with greaseproof paper.

Heat the first 4 ingredients together gently in a pan until the butter has melted, then allow to cool. Mix the dry ingredients in a mixing bowl and make a hollow in the centre. Slowly pour in the melted mixture, stirring all the time so a smooth batter is formed. Beat in the eggs, then stir in the stem ginger and sultanas or raisins.

Pour the mixture into the prepared cake tin and bake in the preheated oven for 1½–2 hours until the cake is well risen and firm in the centre. A cocktail stick inserted into the middle should come out clean. Let the gingerbread cool in the tin.

Store the gingerbread, whole and well wrapped in foil, in an airtight tin, for two days before eating.

A 'cookie shine' is an old Scots word for a tea party. Used mainly in the 19th century, the word is more or less obsolete these days, but I have named this cake after it; it is so full of gorgeous things it is worthy of a party. It would make a wonderful birthday cake. Cookies in Scotland do not mean American biscuits, but round, yeasted, sweet buns, usually either split and filled with cream or iced with (sadly often garishly coloured) icing and known then as iced cookies.

Cookie shine cake

SERVES 8

250g/9 oz self-raising flour
275g/9¾ oz light muscovado sugar
½ teaspoon ground cinnamon
a pinch of salt
2 large free-range eggs, beaten
225ml/8 fl oz sunflower oil
1 × 432g can of crushed pineapple in natural juice, drained
2 small ripe bananas, peeled and mashed
50g/1¾ oz desiccated coconut
75g/2¾ oz chopped roasted hazelnuts

FOR THE ICING
100g/3½ oz butter, softened
1 teaspoon vanilla extract
200g/7 oz cream cheese (low-fat is suitable)
300g/10½ oz golden icing sugar, sifted
1 tablespoon chopped roasted hazelnuts

Preheat the oven to 180°C/350°F/Gas 4. Grease two 20cm/8 in cake tins with butter.

For the cake, mix the flour, sugar, cinnamon and salt together, then add the eggs and oil. Add the pineapple, bananas, coconut and hazelnuts and combine well. Spoon the mixture into the prepared cake tins and bake in the preheated oven for 35–40 minutes or until a skewer inserted into the middle comes out clean. Leave to rest for about 30 minutes, then turn the cakes on to a wire rack to cool.

For the icing, cream the butter, vanilla extract and cream cheese together with an electric beater until smooth, then add the icing sugar a little at a time. Beat again with the electric beater until completely smooth. Use to fill and top the cake. Finally, scatter the hazelnuts over the top.

*Although originally a French delicacy, friands are something
I came across in Australia where they are often served with
'morning tea': I absolutely loved them. Similar to tiny little
sponges, they are light, buttery and – well, just small enough
for you to manage at least two or even three at one sitting. My
recipe was inspired by Luke Mangan's, one of Sydney's top chefs.*

*Make them in shallow bun tins or mini muffin tins – or, best
of all, small oval-shaped moulds.*

*If you cannot find blaeberries (wild bilberries in Scots), then
substitute blueberries instead.*

Blaeberry friands

MAKES about 20

50g/1³⁄₄ oz plain flour
200g/7 oz golden icing sugar
100g/3¹⁄₂ oz ground almonds
140g/5 oz unsalted butter, melted
4 large free-range egg whites
a pinch of salt
110g/4 oz blaeberries

Preheat the oven to 200°C/400°F/Gas 6. Butter about 20 small moulds (see above).

Sift the flour and icing sugar into a bowl, then stir in the almonds. Combine the melted butter with this flour mixture.

Whisk the egg whites with the salt until soft peaks are formed (they must not be stiff). Then fold the egg whites into the mixture, a spoonful at a time. Fold in the berries carefully so they do not bruise.

Spoon the mixture into the prepared moulds and bake in the preheated oven for 15–20 minutes or until puffed up and golden brown. Remove the friands from the oven, and let them rest a little before transferring them from the tin to a wire rack to cool completely.

Whenever we drive down the east coast from Edinburgh, the first stopping place is a little village called Belsay, north of Newcastle: I am gasping for coffee and the children are ready for something delicious to eat. The home-baking at The Blacksmith's Coffee Shop is superb, and it is their Hazelnut Chocolate Shortbread on which I have based my Millionaires' Shortbread recipe. It is utterly divine – admittedly rather rich but deeply satisfying. If you like Snickers bars you will love this!

Incidentally, do not even think about skipping the roasting of the hazelnuts: the difference is unbelievable.

Roasted hazelnut millionaires' shortbread

MAKES 24 pieces

150g/5½ oz whole blanched
   hazelnuts
350g/12 oz plain flour
1 level teaspoon baking powder
175g/6 oz butter, diced
75g/2¾ oz light muscovado sugar
200g/7 oz plain chocolate, melted
   (50–60% cocoa solids)
75g/2¾ oz ground almonds

FOR THE TOPPING

175g/6 oz butter
100g/3½ oz golden caster sugar
2 tablespoons golden syrup
1 × 397g can of condensed milk
225g/8 oz quality plain or
   milk chocolate

Preheat the oven to 170°C/325°F/Gas 3. Place the hazelnuts on a baking sheet and put into the oven as it heats up. They will take up to 15 minutes or so (depending on your oven) to become nicely toasted and golden; the tell-tale sign is when you begin to smell a lovely nutty aroma. Then remove (leaving the oven on) and cool.

Butter a 23 × 33cm/ 9 × 13 in Swiss-roll tin. Sift the flour and baking powder into a bowl and rub in the butter. Stir in the sugar. Now add the melted chocolate and ground almonds, and work in: the result will look rather bitty, not smooth. Tip the mixture into the prepared tin, pressing down the mixture with the palms of your lightly floured hands to ensure it is level. Prick all over then bake in the preheated oven for 40 minutes. Remove from the oven and cool. Scatter the roasted hazelnuts over the top.

For the topping, place the butter, sugar, syrup and condensed milk in a heavy-based saucepan and bring very slowly to the boil, stirring constantly. Bubble away gently, stirring or whisking all the time, until it is pale golden. It is imperative you stir all the time or it will catch and burn. Ignore the phone. Pour the topping over the cooled shortbread, spreading it out evenly. Once cool and set, melt the chocolate and pour over, spreading out carefully to cover. Cut the shortbread into pieces once cold.

Strawberry jam is probably everyone's favourite jam, but many people are extremely wary about making it, for fear of having jars of runny jam. But ever since Jam Sugar (with its added pectin) was invented, the life of the jam maker has been made easier. Instead of adding liquid pectin or lemon juice to compensate for the low pectin in strawberries, you need simply use the same quantities as you do for most jams – i.e. equal fruit to sugar. The other handy thing about strawberry jam made with Jam Sugar is that it is boiled for a mere 4 minutes, unlike raspberry jam which you have to boil for 20 minutes before setting point.

Whole strawberry jam

Scooping out whole strawberries is one of the perks of opening a fresh pot of jam. It is easy to achieve a perfect balance of whole berries suspended in brilliant scarlet jam provided you only mash about half the quantity of berries and also let it stand for 20–30 minutes before actually potting it. Once it is partially cool, the berries sink a little and do not all rise to the surface.

After a day picking strawberries with the children at my local pick-your-own farm, West Craigie at South Queensferry, I like nothing better than to get out my jam pan ('jeelie pan'), and start to make jam immediately for, by that time, we are all heartily sick of the fresh fruit, having put far more into our mouths than our punnets.

To sterilise jam jars, I put them through a full cycle in the dishwasher, and then thoroughly dry them. Just before potting the jam, I warm the jars in the microwave. Alternatively, the jars can be washed, and then thoroughly dried in a low oven for 30 minutes.

MAKES 5 × 350g/12 oz jars

**1kg/2 lb 4 oz fresh strawberries,
   hulled**
**1kg/2 lb 4 oz Jam Sugar
   (with added pectin)**
knob of butter

Place the strawberries in a large saucepan or preserving pan in layers with the sugar and leave for an hour or so, stirring once.

Place the pan over a low heat and, stirring often, heat gently until the sugar dissolves. During this time, mash down about half the berries, leaving the rest whole.

Once the sugar is all dissolved, increase the heat to maximum, add the butter (which disperses the scum) and bring to a full rolling boil (i.e. the mixture rises and cannot be stirred down). Boil like this for 4 minutes, stirring occasionally, until setting point.

After the 4 minutes, remove the pan from the heat and test for setting: place a good dribble of jam on a cold saucer and leave for a minute or two before pushing a finger through it: if the surface wrinkles and a clear line is left through the jam, it is ready. (If not, re-boil for another minute; then test again.)

Leave the jam to stand for about 25 minutes, then stir and pot in warmed, sterilised jars. Wipe the jars clean with a damp cloth. Once they are completely cold, cover tightly and label. Store somewhere cool and dark.

You'll have had your tea?

'YOU'LL HAVE HAD YOUR TEA?' the old Glasgwegian joke used to go. Deriding the alleged inhospitality of Edinburgh's genteel residents, this was yet another case of East–West rivalry, with the two major cities' continual gentle barracking about everything from church, history and architecture to less esoteric causes such as how best to cook mince.

But the point worth explaining about this jest (apart from the fact that, although born in Dundee, I was brought up in Edinburgh and I refute the sentiment entirely) is that tea is not what southerners mean by tea. Tea to those of us in the north of Britain (for it is a term most commonly used in Scotland and northern England) is an evening meal of a savoury course followed by something sweet, with tea drunk throughout: in other words, high tea as opposed to afternoon tea. It was eaten any time from five to six o'clock and kept you going until a little supper – perhaps oatcakes and cheese, or some home-baking – about nine o'clock with your cocoa before bed. Many a time have southerners been duped by the simple invitation to 'tea', ready for a mere cup of tea and cake, to find a full-blown three-course meal and barely a cup of tea in sight. The reverse is also true for us, with obligatory fish suppers *en route* home after an invitation to 'tea' down south!

Traditionally, tea was dishes such as pies, bridies, eggs, smoked fish, and bacon. Nowadays, there are new-fangled things such as salads thrown into tea time (and not just the infamous Glaswegian salad of cold chips doused in vinegar), quiches, soufflés and savoury custards. And although these were traditionally followed by mountains of scones, bannocks and cakes, there is perhaps room these days for a nod towards healthy eating in the form of fruit.

Nowadays, with our long working hours, timings might seem a little early, but the basic concept behind the five o'clock tea time was that the family ate together, before children became hungry and overly tired and when parents had just arrived from work. These days, five o'clock would almost always be a practical impossibility, but I cannot stress enough how passionately I feel about continuing the ritual of the family meal, even if it is eaten a little later in the day. Tea seems like the ideal one to me.

Have you ever wondered what to do with packs of smoked salmon trimmings which are so much cheaper than regular packs of finely sliced and beautifully presented smoked salmon? Here is a way of using them other than in pâtés, pasta sauce and sandwiches.

This is an unusual but very moreish salad, served warm and with a beautifully smoky flavour from the fish. The anchovies give the dressing a nice kick, which is then balanced by the soothing addition of the crème fraîche. This is altogether a simple yet exceedingly tasty salad. And also pretty cheap!

Warm smoked salmon salad

SERVES 6

1 × 50g can of anchovies in oil

1 × 200ml/7 fl oz tub of crème fraîche

200g/7 oz smoked salmon trimmings

15g/½ oz snipped chives

juice of 1 lemon

2 level teaspoons horseradish sauce

freshly ground black pepper

crisp salad leaves
    (cos or little gem)

crusty bread, to serve

Place the anchovies and their oil in a saucepan and heat over a very low heat, stirring to break them up. After 2–3 minutes, add the crème fraîche and slowly bring to the boil. Then simmer, uncovered, for about 5 minutes. Add two-thirds of the smoked salmon and all the chives, and stir well. Return to a low heat and simmer for 2 minutes; then remove from the heat.

Add the lemon juice, horseradish and plenty of pepper to taste. (You should not need salt because of the anchovies and smoked salmon.)

Place the salad leaves in a large shallow salad bowl, pour over the smoked salmon dressing and garnish with the remaining pieces of smoked salmon. Serve at once with bread.

Do try to find Lanark Blue for this recipe (although Roquefort is a possible substitute) as its unique flavour and soft texture make it the best not only for this recipe but for a place on the cheese board in its own right, served perhaps with some good oatcakes and crisp yet ripe pears. Having been put out of production for some months in 1995 because of a ludicrous decision by local health officers, Humphrey Errington in Strathclyde thankfully is still selling his gorgeous cheese not only in Scotland but also down south. We can now salute the return of one of Scotland's finest cheeses. Made from sheep's milk, it is often hailed as 'Scotland's answer to Roquefort', but it is, in fact, in a class of its own.

Lanark blue cheese and walnut salad

SERVES 3–4

75g/2³⁄₄ oz walnuts, toasted

lettuce (including chicory or
   raddicchio), ready prepared

100g/3¹⁄₂ oz Lanark blue,
   roughly chopped or crumbled
   into large chunks

100g/3¹⁄₂ oz small red seedless
   grapes

FOR THE DRESSING

2 tablespoons walnut oil

1 tablespoon sunflower oil

1 tablespoon sherry vinegar

salt and freshly ground black
   pepper

Toasting any nut, whether macadamias, hazelnuts or walnuts, improves them enormously. Simply place the shelled nuts under a grill and, watching carefully, heat until a lovely nutty aroma is evident, or place them in a preheated oven at 170°C/325°F/Gas 3 for about 10 minutes or so.

Arrange the lettuce in a shallow salad dish and top with the walnuts, cheese and grapes.

Shake together – or whisk – the salad dressing. Drizzle over the salad and toss just before serving.

A tarte tatin is not as difficult to make as some people imagine. All you need is a reliable pan (I use a Le Creuset cast-iron one with handles on either side) and a deft touch. When it is time to invert the tart on to the serving dish, invert quickly, then give the pan a good, firm shake – just once – and the tart will emerge from the base on to the dish. If it looks a little ragged, just patch it up.

Asparagus tarte tatin

I like to buy my asparagus from the Pattullos – Heather and Sandy – who have been producing asparagus commercially at Eassie Farm by Glamis in Tayside for some fifteen years. The asparagus season in Scotland generally runs from 8 May until 20 June. Heather's favourite method of cooking asparagus is to boil or steam it, then serve it with hollandaise sauce, although she also likes it roasted with olive oil. Since Pattullo asparagus is all picked at the top of the hard, white part of the stem (unlike some other growers), it requires no peeling. I simply bend it until it snaps to remove the woody end; alternatively, I retain the thick end since it can then be used to hold between fingers and thumb for dipping into a sauce.

Although the most popular asparagus is Select (middle thickness), the Pattullos grade theirs from Sprue (very thin), followed by Choice and Select, then the fattest – Jumbo. For this recipe, I advise using Choice or Select.

The more aged your balsamic vinegar is, the better the final taste will be. You can, of course, use any cheese but I like half Loch Arthur Cheddar and half pecorino.

SERVES 4

FOR THE PASTRY
250g/9 oz plain flour, sifted
125g/4½ oz chilled unsalted
   butter, diced
a pinch of salt
about 4–5 tablespoons cold water

FOR THE FILLING
4 tablespoons olive oil
450g/1 lb onions, peeled and
   sliced very thinly
1 tablespoon balsamic vinegar
salt and freshly ground black
   pepper
300–350g/10½–12 oz asparagus
125g/4½ oz farmhouse cheese,
   coarsely grated or crumbled

For the pastry, place the flour, butter and salt in a food processor and process until it resembles breadcrumbs. Slowly add just enough of the water to form small balls. Remove from the food processor, wrap in clingfilm and chill briefly.

Meanwhile, heat 2 tablespoons of the oil in a saucepan and add the onions. Cook them over a very low heat for about 30 minutes, stirring often, until they are golden and caramelised. Remove the pan from the heat, stir in the vinegar and season with salt and pepper to taste.

Preheat the oven to 220°C/425°F/Gas 7.

Snap off any woody ends from the asparagus and place the spears on an oven tray. Toss them in the remaining oil and roast them at the top of the preheated oven for about 10 minutes or until tender. Reduce the oven temperature to 190°C/375°F/Gas 5.

Oil the base and sides of a 26cm/10½ in tarte tatin dish. Arrange the asparagus spears neatly into the base of the tin; I like to place them side by side, alternating heads and ends.

Cover the asparagus with the onion mixture, then scatter the cheese over the top.

Roll out the pastry to a circle slightly larger than the size of the dish. Place the pastry over the cheese, and carefully tuck it down the sides, all the way round the dish. (Remember, the dish will be inverted to form the crust.)

Bake the tart in the preheated oven for 30–35 minutes, or until a light golden brown. Loosen the edges, allow the tart to rest for 3–4 minutes, then quickly and deftly invert the cooking dish on to the serving dish. Serve warm.

These are really handy little soufflés to have tucked away in your freezer for when you find yourself – as I often do – with a houseful of guests and not wanting to spend hours in the kitchen cooking while missing out not only on pre-prandial drinks but also on any pertinent gossip. For the herb oil, a mixture of any of the following is good: parsley, rocket, basil.

You will need 8 regular-sized ramekins (150ml/5 fl oz capacity), well buttered.

Smoked haddock soufflés with herb oil

SERVES 4 as main course;
8 as starter

500g/1 lb 2 oz undyed smoked
haddock fillets
350ml/12 fl oz full-fat milk
40g/1½ oz butter
40g/1½ oz plain flour
salt and freshly ground black
pepper
40g/1½ oz freshly grated
Parmesan
4 large free-range eggs, separated

FOR THE HERB OIL
25g/1 oz fresh herbs (see above)
about 6 tablespoons extra virgin
olive oil
dash of lemon juice
salt and pepper

Place the fish in a pan with the milk and bring slowly to the boil. After simmering for 2 minutes, remove it from the heat, cover and leave for about 30 minutes. Then drain over a sieve, reserving the liquid.

Melt the butter in a pan and add the flour, stirring well. Cook for about 1 minute, then gradually add the flavoured milk and cook, whisking or stirring constantly, over a medium heat for about 3 minutes until thick. Season with salt and pepper to taste. Stir in the Parmesan and then the egg yolks, one at a time.

Flake the fish into large chunks, being careful to remove any bones, and add to the mixture.

Whisk the egg whites with a pinch of salt until stiff. Carefully fold into the fish mixture one large spoonful at a time. Divide the mixture between the 8 buttered ramekins (see above) and wipe the rims clean (spillage will inhibit even rising). Wrap in clingfilm and freeze just as soon as possible although you may have to wait for a minute or two for them to cool.

Preheat the oven to 200°C/400°F/Gas 6.

The herb oil is best made on the day you are going to eat the soufflés. Process the herbs with the oil in a small blender. Add the lemon juice and salt and pepper to taste.

Shortly before you are ready to eat, remove the clingfilm and place the ramekins on a baking sheet and cook them, still frozen, in the preheated oven for 25–30 minutes until they are puffed up and golden brown. Break open the soufflés with a teaspoon, spoon in some herb oil and serve at once.

Finnan haddock – named after the village of Findon, south of Aberdeen – is a traditionally smoked haddock. Cold-smoked, it needs only gentle poaching to be cooked lightly before being added to all sorts of dishes from pastas and kedgerees to pies and mousses. If you cannot find finnan haddock, then use the equivalent weight of regular fillets of smoked haddock but do be sure to buy the undyed fish.

Lovage is an old-fashioned herb that works perfectly with smoked fish, bacon or smoked ham. If you cannot get fresh lovage, try chives or some chopped celery leaves.

Finnan haddock and lovage tart

SERVES 4–6

FOR THE PASTRY
200g/7 oz plain flour, sifted
25g/1 oz fine oatmeal or polenta
125g/4½ oz unsalted butter, diced
a pinch of salt
1 large free-range egg, beaten
olive oil

FOR THE FILLING
1 finnan haddock (weighing about 350–400g/12–14 oz)
200ml/7 fl oz milk
150ml/5 fl oz double cream
2 large free-range eggs
2 tablespoons freshly chopped lovage
salt and freshly ground black pepper

For the pastry, place the flour, oatmeal or polenta, butter and salt in a food processor and process briefly, then slowly add the egg through the feeder tube. If the dough looks rather bitty, you could add a teaspoon of oil, then bring the dough together with your hands and wrap it in clingfilm. Chill the dough for an hour or so, then roll out to fit a buttered 28cm/11 in shallow tart tin. Prick the base and chill again – preferably overnight.

Preheat the oven to 190°C/375°F/Gas 5.

The pastry should be baked blind (filled with foil and baking beans) in the preheated oven for 15 minutes. Remove the foil and beans, and continue to bake for a further 5 minutes. Remove the tart from the oven (leaving the oven on) and allow it to cool.

Poach the haddock in the milk for 4–5 minutes. Drain the fish through a sieve into a large jug or mixing bowl, reserving the liquid. To the liquid, add the cream, eggs and lovage and season to taste with salt and pepper. (I know it doesn't seem very pleasant tasting raw custard but it is essential, because some curing of finnan haddock is saltier than others.)

Flake the haddock into the tart case and slowly pour over the filling. Bake in the preheated oven for 30–40 minutes or until set and tinged with golden brown. Eat warm with salad.

YOU'LL HAVE HAD YOUR TEA?

This is one of my fishmonger Gavin Borthwick's favourite suppers. He serves the fish with noodles tossed in the parsleyed pan juices. A salad on the side would be nice, if a little un-Scottish!

Other suitable fish would be plaice or dab. Ask your fishmonger to scale, trim and clean the fish for you.

Pan-fried lemon sole with noodles

SERVES 2

1 tablespoon olive oil

40g/1 1/2 oz butter

2 lemon sole (each about 400g/ 14 oz)

salt and freshly ground black pepper

200g/7 oz egg noodles

2 heaped tablespoons finely chopped parsley

lemon wedges, to serve

Heat the oil in a large frying pan. Once hot, add the butter.

Season the fish with salt and pepper and, when the pan is almost smoking, add one fish, dark side down. Shake the pan a little so the skin doesn't stick. Leave (without touching it at all) for about 1 1/2 minutes, then carefully turn over the fish.

Cook for a further 1 1/2–2 1/2 minutes : you can test that it is ready by prodding near the bone with the tip of a sharp knife. Remove the sole with a fish slice to a warm plate and keep warm. Cook the other fish in the same way and place on a second warm plate, keeping the pan to one side.

Meanwhile, cook the noodles according to the instructions on the packet, and then drain.

Add the parsley to the fish pan, increase the heat, then tip in the noodles, tossing them to ensure they are coated in the lovely buttery parsley juices. Serve the noodles with the sole and garnish with lemon wedges.

A variation on the classic dish of herrings in oatmeal, this is really delicious. It makes a very cheap dish for tea or supper, so splash out and serve with a really good bottle of white wine. The Scottish herring season has become shorter and shorter over the years (it is now primarily June, July and August) but when there is a chance to buy them from the west coast, my family feasts on them.

Herrings in couscous

SERVES 3

115g/4 oz couscous
juice of 3 small or 2 large lemons
**salt and freshly ground black
    pepper**
**1 heaped tablespoon freshly
    chopped mint**
3 small herrings, filleted
olive oil

Preheat the oven to 200°C/400°F/Gas 6.

Place the couscous in a bowl and squeeze over the lemon juice. Leave to soak for 10 minutes or so, then fork it through and season with salt and pepper to taste. Stir in the mint.

Lay out the 6 herring fillets on a board, skin-side down, and dampen the flesh with a tiny splash of water (this helps the couscous adhere; alternatively, swish lightly under the tap).

Now press the flesh side into the couscous and lay each fillet, couscous-side up, on an oiled baking tray. Bake in the preheated oven for 15 minutes or until the flesh is just cooked. Meanwhile preheat the grill.

Flash the tray under the grill in order to make the couscous slightly golden and crunchy. Serve piping hot with a lightly dressed rocket salad and some ciabatta.

Fish pie is one of those wonderfully versatile dishes that can be served at either the family tea or a friends' supper party. I like to use a mixture of smoked haddock and fresh fish and, although I usually get my fishmonger's advice on what is available, a good choice is smoked haddock, fresh haddock, cod, coley or hoke. I use smoked haddock for half the quantity and then a selection of fresh fish to make up the other half.

Serve with peas, or with a sorrel and watercress salad.

Fish pie with haddock, capers and dill

SERVES 6

1.1kg/2 lb 7 oz skinned fish fillets
   (see above)
450ml/16 fl oz whole milk
25g/1 oz dill, both stalks and fronds
8–10 peppercorns
salt
50g/1¾ oz butter
50g/1¾ oz plain flour
100ml/3½ fl oz dry white wine or
   vermouth
3 heaped tablespoons capers
zest of 1 large unwaxed lemon
3 large free-range eggs, hard-
   boiled and shelled

FOR THE TOPPING

1.25kg/2¾ lb large potatoes,
   peeled and halved
salt and freshly ground black
   pepper
50g/1¾ oz butter
1 tablespoon extra virgin olive oil
25g/1 oz freshly grated Parmesan

Place the fish in a large saucepan with the milk. Break off the dill stalks and add these with the peppercorns. Bring slowly to the boil, bubble for 1 minute, then remove from the heat, cover and leave for 30 minutes or so.

For the topping, boil the potatoes in salted water until tender, then drain thoroughly. Mash them with the butter and oil, then add the cheese and season to taste.

Strain the fish over a bowl reserving the liquor, discard the dill and peppercorns, break the fish into large chunks and place in a large ovenproof dish.

In another saucepan, melt the butter, then add the flour. Cook, stirring, for 1–2 minutes, then gradually add the wine or vermouth and the fish liquor, whisking constantly until the sauce is smooth and thickened. Cook for 5 minutes or so, then remove the pan from the heat and add the capers and lemon zest. Chop the dill, add to the mixture, taste and check for seasoning. Slice the eggs, place over the fish, then pour over the sauce. Top with the potato, first smoothing the top, then forking it up to make a rough surface. Either cook and eat now, or cover with clingfilm and chill overnight. If you are cooking it the next day, be sure to bring it to room temperature first.

Preheat the oven 190°C/375°F/Gas 5. Put the pie on a baking tray (in case of spillage) and cook in the preheated oven for about 1 hour, until golden brown and bubbling. Leave for at least 5 minutes before serving.

This is one of those most perfect food combinations, like bacon and eggs or strawberries and cream. It is a delicious summer treat and is the perfect contrast of textures, taste and expense, with lobster being regarded as a luxury and chips most certainly not. The mayonnaise somehow bridges the gap between extravagance and everyday.

Eat this, preferably outside, on a warm summer's evening.

Lobster, chips and mayo

SERVES 2

1 lobster (or 2 small), freshly boiled (see page 90)
chip-shop chips

FOR THE MAYONNAISE
2 medium free-range egg yolks
1 teaspoon Dijon mustard
juice of 1 lemon, freshly squeezed
salt and freshly ground black pepper
about 300ml/10 fl oz oil (half sunflower, half olive)

First prepare the mayo: place the egg yolks, mustard, 1 teaspoon lemon juice and plenty of salt and pepper in a food processor and process for a few seconds. Then very slowly dribble in the oil through the feeder tube, literally drop by drop at first. Once an emulsion has begun to form, you can increase the dribble to a thin, slow stream.

Spoon the mayo into a bowl and add ½ tablespoon boiling water in order to thin the mayo a little. Taste again and add salt and pepper – and extra lemon juice, if you like.

While your fellow diner nips off to the chippy, you can begin tackling the lobster. Place the lobster, shell uppermost, on a board on the table in front of you. Cut down the middle, along the length of the lobster, then remove and discard the stomach sac (which looks like crumpled clingfilm), the dark intestinal thread running down the tail and the greyish feathery gills. Everything else is edible. Place the two halves of lobster on to plates. Now you must simply wait for your chip delivery; you could usefully uncork a bottle of good white wine and perhaps check that it is drinkable.

When your fellow diner returns with the chips, decant them on to hot plates and place them alongside the lobster, together with the bowl of mayo. Bash the lobster's claws open or poke out the meat with lobster picks – crochet hooks will do just as well. Remove the main tail meat, then suck at the legs to extract every last morsel of meat. Eat hot chips alternately with chunks of lobster, both dunked in mayo.

Did I mention that one bottle of wine will not be enough?

Isle of Mull cheese is a sharp, powerful Cheddar-style cheese that is made in the old-fashioned way from unpasteurised milk on the Isle of Mull off the west coast of Scotland. If you cannot get it, use a good farmhouse Cheddar instead.

This savoury bread and butter pudding is absolutely wonderful – but don't even consider slinging in the contents of your fridge to use up ends of things. It relies on good-quality ingredients, from bread to ham and cheese. For the bread, I like to use sourdough.

Isle of Mull cheese and ham bread-and-butter pudding

SERVES 6

150–175g/5¹/₂–6 oz bread, sliced thickly, crusts left on

70g/2¹/₂ oz butter, softened

Dijon mustard

175g/6 oz quality ham, roughly chopped

125g/4¹/₂ oz Isle of Mull cheese, coarsely grated

600ml/1 pint milk

5 large free-range eggs

salt and freshly ground black pepper

1 tablespoon freshly chopped parsley

Butter a 2 litre/3¹/₂ pint ovenproof dish and preheat the oven to 180°C/350°F/Gas 4.

Spread the bread thickly with the butter, then thinly with the mustard. Place half the slices in the base of the prepared dish. Top with the ham and half the cheese, then with the remaining bread, buttered-side up.

Whisk together the milk and eggs and season with salt and pepper. Add the parsley, then slowly pour the mixture over the bread, taking care to soak it all over. Scatter the remaining cheese on top. Leave to soak in for at least 20 minutes.

Put the dish in a bain-marie (or a roasting tin filled halfway up the sides with hand-hot water). Bake in the preheated oven for 60–70 minutes, or until puffed up and golden brown.

Ayrshire bacon is traditionally brine-cured. It is similar to Wiltshire bacon but, unlike Wiltshire bacon which is brine-cured with the rind on and the bones in, sides of Ayrshire bacon are cured with the rind off and the bones out. The most popular cut is the middle cut which is a nicely rounded rasher caused by the fact that, after curing and maturing, it is rolled before being smoked (although it can also be bought unsmoked or green) and sliced.

Serve this lovely and simple high tea dish with a well-dressed rocket salad and some thick slices of chewy bread, Italian for preference.

Pan-fried mozzarella wrapped in Ayrshire bacon

SERVES 2

**2 balls of mozzarella
(each weighing about
125–150g/4¹/₂–5¹/₂ oz)**
salt and freshly ground pepper
**4–5 rashers of Ayrshire middle
bacon**
olive oil
**rocket salad and good bread,
to serve**

With kitchen paper, pat the cheeses completely dry, then season with salt and pepper. Wrap each cheese in bacon; use 2–2¹/₂ rashers per ball since you want as much of the cheese covered as possible.

Heat a little oil in a frying pan (just enough to cover the surface once it is swirled around) and when it is hot, add the mozzarella parcels. Leave for at least 1 minute before carefully turning them over. After 3–4 minutes, they should be nicely crisp all over.

To serve, pile some rocket salad onto plates and top with a hot bacon-wrapped mozzarella ball. Drizzle over the pan juices and serve at once with plenty of warm bread.

YOU'LL HAVE HAD YOUR TEA?

This combination is utterly divine – juicy, tender slices of steak sitting atop an interesting and colourful salad, with a whole shucked oyster nestling on top. This is a far cry from pie, beans and chips for tea but, for a treat, there is little to beat this delicious salad which should be eaten with some warm, crusty bread.

Steak and oyster salad

SERVES 4

4 rib-eye steaks

2 tablespoons oyster sauce

2 red peppers, quartered and seeded

4 tablespoons olive oil

1 tablespoon red wine vinegar

salt and freshly ground black pepper

peppery salad leaves (watercress, rocket)

4 oysters

Marinate the steaks in the oyster sauce for an hour or so.

Meanwhile, preheat the grill. Place the peppers skin-side up on a sheet of foil on a grill tray, and heat under the grill for 5–10 minutes, until the skins are charred and blistered. Remove the peppers and tightly wrap in foil. Leave for 10–15 minutes while the skin is loosened, then remove the skin and wipe the pepper with kitchen paper. Cut into slivers.

Make the dressing by shaking together the oil, vinegar and salt and pepper in a screw-top jar. Put the salad in a bowl with the red pepper, and add the dressing, tossing to coat. Pile some on to each plate.

Next shuck the oysters: wrap your left hand in a tea towel (assuming you are right handed) and place an oyster, cup-side down, hinge towards you, in your palm. Insert an oyster knife or small, sharp knife into the hinge. Push and twist simultaneously, passing the knife under the top shell to cut the muscle and sliding it along the length to open fully. Leave the now loose oyster in its shell, retaining all the juices.

Heat a little oil in a frying pan until very hot, add the steaks and cook on a high heat for 4–5 minutes, turning once; this will produce them medium-rare. Remove and rest for 5 minutes.

Slice the steaks diagonally into thick slices and place on top of the salad leaves. Top each with an oyster in its shell.

The smell of these bridies fills the house with fabulous aromas that not only make you want to stop everything and devour one the minute it has finished cooking, you also want to bless the person that invented the bridie.

Venison Bridies

There are various tales about the etymology of the word, from the story that they were baked for brides on their wedding day to the slightly more plausible tale of one Margaret Bridie of Glamis who sold horseshoe-shaped meat pies in Forfar market. The horseshoe shape (they are not half moons like the Cornish pastie) meant they became a lucky symbol, served at weddings and christenings. Whatever historical significance, the Forfar bridie – to my mind – is a thing of glory, if properly executed, and I reckon some of the best are from James McLaren & Sons, bakers in Forfar, where I learned the famous 'dunting and nicking' techniques.

The venison bridie is equally delicious and mouth-watering. Enjoy with a glass of red wine and a salad, both of which are, of course, untraditional accompaniments.

MAKES 4

FOR THE PASTRY

250g/9 oz strong white flour

75g/2¾ oz plain flour

½ teaspoon salt

175g/6 oz unsalted butter, cubed

about 3 tablespoons cold water

FOR THE FILLING

500g/1 lb 2 oz venison, coarsely minced (usually taken from the shin)

75g/2¾ oz beef suet, grated

1 small onion, peeled and finely grated

1 heaped tablespoon freshly chopped parsley

salt and freshly ground black pepper

For the pastry, sift the flours and salt into a food processor. Add the butter and process until it is incorporated. Add just enough of the water to bind it to a stiff dough. Gather the dough in your hands, wrap it in clingfilm and chill for at least 1 hour.

For the filling, mix the venison, suet, onion and parsley and season well with salt and pepper.

Divide the pastry into four and roll each piece into an oval. Divide the filling into four and spoon it onto the top half of each pastry oval, leaving a border round the edges.

Dampen the edges, then fold the other half of the pastry over the filling to enclose it. Trim the edges into a neat horseshoe shape. Now 'dunt' and 'nick' by pressing down the edges to seal them and crimping right round to give a nicely finished look. Using a sharp knife, prick a small hole in the top of each bridie; this allows the steam to escape. Place the bridies on a lightly buttered baking tray and chill for an hour or so.

Meanwhile, preheat the oven to 200°C/400°F/Gas 6.

Bake in the preheated oven for 35–40 minutes or until golden brown. Serve the bridies warm, not hot.

Soup on the hills

MY UNCLE FRANK (known as Unc in the family) has been going to the hills almost every weekend for the past sixty-eight years. In his youth, he would get on his bike in Dundee, where he lived with his brother – my father – and two sisters, and cycle to one of the Angus glens (Glens Clova, Isla or Prosen), deposit the bike at a bothy and walk in the hills. It was 1936 when he first took my father, Bob, along with him (my dad was only thirteen at the time) and after the thirty-five-mile cycle to Glen Isla they stayed the night in a bothy, returning the next day.

For my father's debut on the hills, tinned soup was taken in knapsacks and heated up over a primus stove in the bothy. When I asked why home-made soup was not taken in a thermos (surely home-made soup was cheaper? And every Scottish home had a pot of soup on the go, all year long), he said thermos flasks were expensive and also rather fragile so it was better to take a tin. Other victuals taken were corned beef sandwiches and a block of dates for instant energy.

Unc still goes to the hills – now aged eighty-three – every second weekend, whether to the Angus glens or further north to Rannoch Moor or Glencoe. These days, he doesn't bicycle and the food taken is mainly sandwiches, chocolate biscuits and thermos flasks of hot coffee or tea. In the winter, however, a thermos of hot soup is essential.

Because thermos flasks, fortunately, are now neither fragile nor expensive, I highly recommend hot soup for long walks, even during the summer: it is not only in Scotland that you can set out for a summer hill walk wearing shorts and T-shirt, and by midday run into thick freezing fog. That is quite simply mountain life.

Some of the soups in this chapter are rather too thick for thermos flasks on the hills, but they are the perfect dish to come home to, after a fresh, bracing day outdoors. Yank off your boots and tuck into a bowl of restorative, warming soup – having poured yourself an appropriate drink. Whisky, of course.

Traditionally, butter beans are often used in the Scottish kitchen – both in soups and as a vegetable beside a plate of everyday mince and tatties. This soup is a beautifully flavoured bean soup topped with some grated Scottish Cheddar-style cheese. I purée only about half the beans: this gives a natural thickness to the soup but leaves some whole beans for texture.

If you cannot find Loch Arthur cheese (a young organic Scottish Cheddar made in Dumfriesshire; milder than English styles), then opt instead for Isle of Mull Cheddar or Dunlop. The latter is a traditionally made cloth-bound cheese from Ayrshire and the former is one of my all-time favourites, sharper in flavour than English Cheddars but truly distinctive. All three are unpasteurised.

This is the sort of soup that will put hairs on your chest … or at least warm you up on a cold day out on the hills.

Butter bean and rosemary soup with Loch Arthur cheese

SERVES 6

350g/12 oz dried butter beans

2 tablespoons olive oil

1 large onion, peeled and chopped

3 garlic cloves, peeled and chopped

1.2 litres/2 pints hot chicken stock

2 thick sprigs of rosemary

salt and freshly ground black pepper

50g/1¾ oz Loch Arthur cheese, coarsely grated, to serve

extra virgin olive oil, to serve

Soak the beans overnight, then drain and rinse.

Heat the olive oil in a saucepan and gently fry the onion and garlic for 10 minutes. Then add the beans, hot stock and rosemary sprigs and season with black pepper (but no salt yet). Bring to the boil, then cover and simmer gently for about 1 hour or until the beans are tender.

Remove the rosemary (and try to extract any leaves which may have dropped off). Using a hand-held electric blender, purée about half the soup, ensuring that some beans are left whole. Now add salt – and more pepper, if necessary – according to taste.

To serve, ladle the soup into warm bowls, and top each bowl with some of the cheese and a drizzle of the oil.

This is a warming, delicious soup served with some rustic croûtons on top, which makes it a meal in itself. Perfect for a winter day.

When making the croûtons, I prefer to tear the bread roughly rather than cube it neatly.

Chick pea and thyme soup with croûtons

SERVES 6

500g/1 lb 2 oz dried chick peas
3 tablespoons olive oil
1 large onion, peeled and
chopped
2–3 thick sprigs of fresh thyme
2 sticks of celery, chopped
2 large garlic cloves, peeled
and chopped
salt and freshly ground black
pepper

FOR THE CROÛTONS
3 tablespoons olive oil
2–3 thick slices of ciabatta,
torn into croûtons
1 sprig of thyme
extra virgin olive oil,
to serve

Soak the chick peas overnight in cold water.

Next day, rinse the chick peas (and pick over, discarding any dark ones), then place them in a large, heavy saucepan. Pour in enough cold water to cover by some 5cm/2 in – about 2 litres/3$\frac{1}{2}$ pints. Bring to the boil, removing any scum with a slotted spoon.

Meanwhile, heat the oil in a frying pan and gently fry the onion and thyme sprigs for about 3 minutes, then add the celery and garlic and fry gently for a further 5 minutes.

Add the contents of the frying pan to the pan of chick peas and bring to the boil. Then lower the heat, cover and simmer for about 3 hours, or until the chick peas are tender. Top up the liquid level every hour, adding enough boiling water to cover the chick peas.

Remove the herb sprigs (don't worry if the leaves have fallen off), then put 4 large ladlefuls of the soup (which will be very thick at this stage) into a blender or food processor with 2 ladlefuls of very hot water. Whiz until you have a purée, then return this to the pan of chick pea soup. (If your food processor has a small bowl, do this in two batches to avoid spillage.)

Season with 2 teaspoons salt and plenty of pepper. Then reheat the soup which will be half purée, half chunky chick peas.

Meanwhile, make the croûtons: heat the oil in a frying pan and add the bread and the thyme sprig. Fry for 3–4 minutes, turning, until golden brown. Drain on kitchen paper and discard the thyme.

To serve, check the soup again for seasoning, then ladle it into 6 bowls. Top with some croutons, then drizzle each with a little of the olive oil.

Lentil soup was one of my childhood staples and I used to love it, thick, warming and satisfying. This version has the addition of roasted garlic which gives a lovely background hint of smoky garlic without any of that potent aftertaste of the raw variety. Don't feel you have to put on your oven especially to roast 4 or 5 cloves of garlic, however: I slip them in to roast after I have made a cake for tea or cooked lasagne for supper. We are not known as thrifty for nothing in Scotland. Once the roasted garlic flesh has been squeezed out, it can be covered and refrigerated for 2–3 days before being used in the soup.

Although this is wonderful served just as it is, a garnish of some chunks of hot-smoked trout and a drizzle of extra virgin olive oil makes it even more delicious.

Lentil and roasted garlic soup

SERVES 4–6

4 fat garlic cloves, unpeeled
25g/1 oz butter
1 tablespoon olive oil
**1 large onion, peeled and
  chopped**
3 sticks of celery, chopped
350g/12 oz red lentils, rinsed
1 bay leaf
**1.5 litres/2³⁄₄ pints hot chicken
  stock**
**salt and freshly ground black
  pepper**

Preheat the oven to 180°C/350°F/Gas 4.

Place the garlic cloves in a small oven dish and roast them in the preheated oven for about 20 minutes or until soft. Remove them when cool enough to handle, snip open the end and squeeze out the contents into a small bowl. Set aside.

Heat the butter and oil in a large saucepan and gently fry the onion and celery for 10 minutes or so, then stir in the roasted garlic and the lentils. Stir well to coat in the fat, then add the bay leaf and hot stock. Bring to the boil, season well with salt and pepper, then cover and simmer for about 25 minutes or until the lentils are cooked. Remove the bay leaf.

Liquidise the soup in batches, returning it to a clean pan, check the seasoning and serve piping hot.

I first ate nettle soup in Finland, where foraging is a way of life. Back home, I often make this soup in early spring when the nettles are young and tender and serve it in the Finnish way, with a hard-boiled egg floating on top.

When you pick nettles, I need hardly say that you will need rubber gloves and scissors (and welly boots unless you have long trousers). Only remove the tops and upper leaves and do not pick from plants that are in flower. Obviously, pick as far away from the roadside as possible.

Nettle soup

And just in case you are wondering, once they are cooked, the sting (formic acid) disappears completely; all you are left with is a wonderfully rich yet sharp flavour not unlike sorrel. Just like sorrel and spinach, nettles cook very quickly and in order to retain their vivid colour, I blanch them shortly after returning home and then purée them. The resulting purée will last in the fridge for 2–3 days which means that you don't have to finish making the soup immediately. The purée can even be used as a stuffing for pasta such as ravioli or cannelloni, mixed with some ricotta and a little fresh mint.

SERVES 6

**250g/9 oz young nettles (roughly
1 full supermarket carrier bag)**

**2 heaped tablespoons freshly
grated Parmesan**

7–8 tablespoons olive oil

**600g/1 lb 5 oz potatoes, peeled
and chopped into chunks**

**1 large onion, peeled and
chopped**

2 sticks of celery, chopped

**1.2 litres/2 pints chicken
(or vegetable) stock**

**salt and freshly ground black
pepper**

**3 large free-range eggs,
hard-boiled and shelled**

First put on your rubber gloves again, and remove the leaves from their stalks, discarding the latter. Put the leaves in a large colander and wash them really well, in several changes of water.

Bring a large pan of water to the boil and, once boiling, drop in all the nettle leaves. When it has returned to the boil, blanch the nettles for 1 minute, then tip them into the colander and refresh under a cold running tap. Drain really well, squeezing them by hand and then patting them dry on kitchen paper. Place in a small food processor. Add the Parmesan and enough of the oil to make a thick purée. Put the purée into a bowl and, if necessary, cover and refrigerate for 2–3 days.

When you are ready to make the soup, place the potatoes in a pan with the onion, celery and stock. Bring to the boil and cook until the vegetables are tender. Then remove the pan from the heat and add the nettle purée. Mix in a blender (or by using a hand-held blender), and season with salt and pepper to taste. Add a little extra boiling water if it is too thick.

If you have to reheat, do not boil the soup or the lovely bright green colour will fade. To serve, ladle the soup into wide bowls and top each with half a hard-boiled egg. Grind over some black pepper and serve.

Although this is inherently a summer soup using seasonal fresh peas, it can also be made at other times of the year using frozen peas. Do not defrost them before cooking.

Instead of mint, you could use chervil or tarragon.

Summer pea soup with mint

SERVES 4

50g/1³⁄₄ oz butter

**1 large onion, peeled and
    chopped**

**about 1.25kg/2³⁄₄ lb peas in the
    pod (or about 500g/
    1 lb 2 oz frozen peas)**

**1 heaped tablespoon fresh mint
    leaves**

**salt and freshly ground black
    pepper**

**double cream and 4 tiny mint
    sprigs, to serve**

Heat the butter in a saucepan, then gently sauté the onion for about 10 minutes.

Shell the peas, and add to the pan with the mint leaves. Stir well to coat in the butter, then add 750ml/25 fl oz boiling water. Bring the contents back to the boil, then reduce to a simmer and cook, covered, for 8–10 minutes until the peas are tender but still a vivid green.

In batches, tip the soup into a liquidiser or blender and purée. Put the soup into a clean pan and season well with salt and pepper to taste. Reheat gently.

Serve the soup in warm bowls, topped with a swirl of cream and a mint sprig.

Fortunately, this gorgeous soup can be made at any time of the year because of the availability of dried wild mushrooms. But if you happen to be picking wild mushrooms, then it is even more sublime. I like it best when made with fresh wild chanterelles (found in the woodlands of Scotland from the end of July until the first frosts of winter), or with dried ceps (porcini). The mushroom flavour is enhanced by the addition of the fresh cultivated mushrooms.

Cream of wild mushroom soup

SERVES 6

250g–300g/9–10¹/₂ oz fresh wild
   mushrooms *or* 50g/1³/₄ oz dried
   wild mushrooms

250ml/9 fl oz dry sherry
   or white wine

50g/1³/₄ oz butter

1 onion, peeled and chopped

3 garlic cloves, peeled and
   chopped

450g/1 lb button or chestnut
   mushrooms, sliced

750ml/25 fl oz hot chicken
   or vegetable stock

salt and freshly ground black
   pepper

150ml/5 fl oz double cream

chopped flat parsley, to serve

If using fresh wild mushrooms, clean them thoroughly by cutting off any root tips and dusting with a soft brush. Slice if very large. If using dried wild mushrooms, rinse them and soak them in the sherry or wine for about 30 minutes.

Melt the butter in a large saucepan and gently fry the onion and garlic for about 10 minutes. Then add both the wild and the cultivated mushrooms: if you are using dried wild mushrooms, they should be drained of their liquor (which should be saved).

Stir well to coat in the butter and cook for a couple of minutes, then add the soaking liquor from the dried mushrooms or, if using fresh, add the sherry or wine. Stir, then cook over a high heat until the liquid has evaporated. Add the stock, season with salt and pepper and bring to the boil. Cover and simmer for about 15 minutes or until tender.

Liquidise in batches, then return to the pan. Reheat gently, add the cream and stir well; check the seasoning one more time. Serve in warm bowls, topped with a scattering of parsley.

The combination of parsnips and Arbroath smokies is, quite simply, divine. It must be something to do with the smokiness of the fish and the inherent sweetness of the parsnips that combine to make the most delicious, warming winter soup imaginable. Too thick and bitty for a thermos flask but delicious in a bowl with a spoon – and some chewy sourdough bread.

Parsnip and cumin soup with smokies

SERVES 6

2 tablespoons olive oil

1 onion, peeled and chopped

2 garlic cloves, peeled and chopped

2 sticks of celery, chopped

2 teaspoons ground cumin

1kg/2¼ lb parsnips, peeled and chopped

1.2 litres/2 pints hot chicken stock

salt and freshly ground black pepper

50ml/2 fl oz Noilly Prat or another dry Vermouth

2 small Arbroath smokies

extra virgin olive oil

1 tablespoon freshly chopped parsley, optional

Heat the oil in a saucepan and gently fry the onion, garlic and celery for about 10 minutes. Add the cumin and cook for half a minute, stirring.

Add the parsnips to the pan, stirring to coat the chunks in the oil. Cook for about 5 minutes, then add the hot stock and some salt and pepper and bring to the boil. Cover and reduce to a simmer and cook for about 25 minutes or until the vegetables are tender.

In batches, tip the contents of the pan into a liquidiser or blender with the Noilly Prat, and purée until smooth; check the seasoning.

Since the Arbroath smokies are hot-smoked, they can be eaten without any further cooking. The easiest way to remove the flesh from the smokies is to warm them slightly first: either do this in a microwave for a couple of minutes, or in a low oven, loosely wrapped in foil, for about 10 minutes. Then lay the fish on a board, skin-side down, and press your thumb along the length of the bone. It should come away easily in your hand and then the flesh can be flaked.

To serve, ladle the soup into bowls, top with some flakes of smokies, drizzle with the oil and sprinkle with parsley, if using.

This makes a quick and simple alternative to Scotland's great cock-a-leekie soup which is classically flavoured with prunes.

Avocado cock-a-leekie

SERVES 4

25g/1 oz butter

1 large chicken breast, skinned, boned and cut into strips

salt and freshly ground black pepper

250g/9 oz young leeks, trimmed, washed and thinly sliced

850ml/1½ pints hot chicken stock

1 large ripe avocado, peeled and sliced

1 tablespoon freshly chopped coriander

Melt the butter in a saucepan. Season the chicken with salt and pepper, then gently fry for 2–3 minutes. Remove with a slotted spoon.

Gently sauté the leeks for 3–4 minutes until tender, then add the hot stock and heat until just below boiling point. Check the seasoning.

To serve, place 2–3 avocado slices in each warmed soup bowl, top with some chicken strips and ladle in the leek soup. Sprinkle with the coriander and serve at once.

This is a wonderfully warming wintry soup, at once thick and comforting. The original idea comes from the time I spent in the north of Finland where, every Thursday, the Finns eat thick pea and mustard soup and pancakes (oven-baked pancake, rather like a sweet Yorkshire pudding) for lunch. This soup, with only four ingredients, couldn't be simpler yet it is absolutely delicious on a cold winter day.

Ask your butcher whether the ham hock requires overnight soaking – some are saltier than others; if in doubt, soak for several hours in cold water.

Winter pea, ham and mustard soup

SERVES 5–6

350g/12 oz dried green split peas
1 ham hock
**1 large onion, peeled and
    chopped**
2 tablespoons Dijon mustard
**salt and freshly ground black
    pepper**

Soak the peas overnight.

Rinse the peas and place them in a large saucepan with the ham hock, onion and mustard. Pour in 1 litre/1^3/$_4$ pints boiling water and plenty of pepper. Cover and bring to the boil, then lower to a simmer and cook for about 50 minutes.

Remove the ham from the pan and drain over a sieve. Once cool enough to handle, cut off chunks of the meat with a sharp knife, and reserve.

Whiz the soup with a hand-held blender (or in a liquidiser) and add salt to taste. Add the chunks of ham to the soup and reheat gently. Serve in warm bowls with an extra dollop of mustard if you like.

Alastair Pearson, proprietor of The Old Inn at Gairloch in the north-west of Scotland, has given me this wonderful recipe which is very popular with guests. The entire emphasis of food at The Old Inn is on fish and game, which makes enormous sense since it nestles at the foot of the Flowerdale Glen, home of the Mackenzie clan, and sits adjacent to Gairloch harbour. His local butcher supplies wild venison from the nearby hills and glens, and local seafood is available in season.

Gairloch Bay chowder with oatcakes

Athough many tourists travelling to the north-west expect an abundance of local seafood in menus, sadly this is not often the case since much of it is contracted to continental markets where it is fully appreciated. Slowly things are improving but it is wonderful to have such unpretentious and inexpensive beacons of culinary excellence as The Old Inn at Gairloch where the importance of sourcing locally is paramount.

This chowder varies according to which seafood is in season but this is a rough guide. It is served at The Old Inn with home-made oatcakes crumbled over the top.

SERVES 4

500g/1 lb 2 oz mussels

3 large potatoes

salt and freshly ground black
   pepper

1 small leek, cleaned and finely
   chopped

1 large onion, peeled and finely
   chopped

25g/1 oz butter (or bacon fat)

600ml/1 pint milk

2 bay leaves

600ml/20 fl oz fish stock

500g/1 lb 2 oz fillets of pollock or
   ling, cut into chunks

150ml/5 fl oz double cream

oatcakes

1 tablespoon freshly chopped
   parsley

Scrub the mussels well, discarding any open ones that don't close when tapped on a work surface.

Peel the potatoes: chop one into chunks and put on to boil in salted water. Dice the other two. Then sweat the leek, onion and potatoes in the butter or bacon fat for about 10 minutes.

Meanwhile, warm the milk with the bay leaves, then add to the pan with the fish stock. Add the mussels, bring to the boil, cover and simmer for about 3 minutes or until the mussels are opened. Remove the mussels and take the meat out of the shells. Set aside, discarding any that have remained closed.

Mash the (third) boiled potato and add it, with the fish fillets and the double cream, to the milk and stock mixture. Bring to a simmer, stir, then cook gently for about 3 minutes or until the fish is just cooked. Return the mussel meat to the pan and check the seasoning.

Serve in warm bowls with broken-up pieces of oatcakes sprinkled over the top. Top with the parsley and serve at once.

A lochside picnic

THE PICNIC HAMPER IS PACKED and, in fact, so full that another basket is needed for cups, knives and glasses. The cool box is loaded with bottles and the thermos flask filled. The car boot is open and everyone is standing around proffering advice on how to jam everything in around the travel rugs, ground sheets, wellies and inflatable dinghy. Someone runs off to the corner shop for the Sunday papers and then the final picnic essential, a hot pie still on the baking tray straight from the oven, is carefully wedged on the back shelf. This will fill the car with glorious smells all the way to Loch Earn.

This is not an expedition into the unknown but just a family picnic to the Highlands. But the preparations and organising require military precision. Oh, I almost forgot: the pie is not, in fact, the last of the victuals. A huge ham sandwich, wrapped in bags and towels, which must be sat upon all the way there. Which child wants the honour today? Faith or Jessica – OK, begin the sitting.

A Lawrence family picnic does not involve neatly cut sandwiches and a flask of tea taken on dinky little chairs by the side of the road (you know the type, we pass them en route). It is a (usually fraught) journey of over an hour, driving north through increasingly beautiful scenery until finally the loch is before us, and our picnic site is chosen. As those of you who are picnic aficionados will attest, the actual choosing of the site is crucial – was it the same as last time, did other picnickers have the audacity to leave litter? Is the water looking too choppy for the dinghy?

Once the site is established, I assume the motherly role (for I am she) of arranging ground sheets, travel rugs and picnic hampers while the children are sent off to collect firewood for the all-essential fire. Pat, my husband, inflates the dinghy and very soon the first cry of 'I'm hungry' is heard – usually from Euan. Any excuse to get out of the hunt for kindling.

Out come the picnic loaves, pâté, cheese, salad, rolls. The pie is still just warm and the squashed ham sandwich perfectly squashed. The fruit cake is cut, the wine opened. All is well with the world.

Lochside picnics – memories are made of these.

This variation on the classic Middle Eastern hummus made with chick peas is a real treat in the summer when it is pea-podding time. But once you have made it, you will find yourself returning to it in winter as well, and using frozen peas; it is so divine. It is also wonderful made with fresh broad beans – but do take the time to slip off their skins after they are cooked and before processing.

Serve this at picnics or bonfires with freshly baked damper bread (page 104), or for supper with warmed Turkish flat breads.

Fresh pea hummus

SERVES 6

900g/2 lb pea pods (or 300g/
   10½ oz frozen petit pois)
2 garlic cloves, peeled and
   crushed
1 heaped teaspoon ground cumin
juice of 1 large lemon
about 5 tablespoons extra virgin
   olive oil
2 tablespoons tahini
salt and freshly ground black
   pepper
paprika or flat parsley, to garnish

Pod the peas and cook until just tender (or cook from frozen); drain and run immediately under the cold tap to arrest cooking. Pat thoroughly dry on kitchen paper.

Tip the peas into a food processor with the remaining ingredients except the paprika or parsley and whiz, then taste, adding more salt, pepper, oil or lemon juice if needed.

Tip the purée into a bowl and garnish with a dusting of paprika or flat parsley leaves.

The last time I drove north to the wilds of Aberdeenshire to stay at Blaimore House near Huntly, I returned with an enormous basket of chanterelles. Our genial host, Hans Baumann, had picked them the day before in the mossy woodlands near Tomintoul in Strathspey. Once I had made soup and served them sautéed with a touch of garlic on toast, I converted the remaining chanterelles (the smaller ones) into a preserve by cooking them in a mixture of vinegar and water, then layering them with bay leaf and garlic and covering in olive oil. The method is based on that employed in the Italian Funghi sott' olio *– mushrooms under oil – which is used throughout Italy to preserve mushrooms so they can be eaten all the year round.*

Chanterelles in olive oil

Since the first of the chanterelles appears in July in Scotland, these are ideal to take on picnics in late summer. Fork out a few and drop them onto some good Italian bread, then drizzle over a little of the olive oil from the jar. For home eating, fork out some of the mushrooms and either eat them as part of an antipasti platter, or place them on bruschetta, flavoured with a smear of garlic and a suggestion of sea salt. Again, use the oil from the jar to drizzle over.

I find it best to keep the chanterelles whole if possible, which is I why I keep back the smaller ones. They should be cleaned, and their root tips trimmed.

MAKES 1 × 500ml/18 fl oz jar

400ml/14 fl oz white wine vinegar

1 small unwaxed lemon

6 bay leaves

400g/14 oz fresh chanterelles

about 300ml/10 fl oz extra virgin
  olive oil

3 garlic cloves, peeled and halved

Place the vinegar in a saucepan with the pared peel of the lemon and 3 of the bay leaves. Add 200ml/7 fl oz cold water and bring to the boil. Once the liquid is bubbling, add the mushrooms and simmer for about 10 minutes, or until tender.

Drain them, then spread them out on clean tea towels to dry. Help to dry them by patting them gently dry with wads of kitchen paper. They are ready to use only when they are completely dry.

Sterilise a 500ml/18 fl oz preserving jar and ensure it is thoroughly dry and cold (see page 38).

Pour some of the oil into the jar, then add a third of the mushrooms, then a bay leaf and half a garlic clove. Cover with more oil, then repeat the layers again, using up all the mushrooms. Add enough oil to cover the mushrooms completely.

Seal the jar well and store somewhere cool – and preferably in the dark – for at least 1 week and for up to 4 weeks.

The easiest way to take this tart to a picnic is to transport it in the baking tin otherwise it will break up. Make the tart the night before or – even better – on the morning of your picnic and take it, still warm, in the car. By the time you arrive at your picnic spot, you will be positively salivating.

If you want to serve it with something extra, a dollop of chilli-spiked mayonnaise goes down a treat.

Crab tart with chilli pastry

SERVES 6–8

FOR THE PASTRY
200g/7 oz plain flour, sifted
1 teaspoon chilli powder
50g/1¾ oz freshly grated
    Parmesan
150g/5½ oz unsalted butter, diced
a pinch of salt
1 medium free-range egg, beaten
a little olive oil, if needed

FOR THE FILLING
450g/1 lb crabmeat
    (mainly white meat)
4 medium free-range eggs
juice of 1 lemon
a pinch of chilli powder
200ml/7 fl oz crème fraîche
salt and freshly ground black
    pepper

For the pastry, place the first 5 ingredients in a food processor. Process briefly, then, with the machine running, add the egg and olive oil, if necessary. Bring the dough together with your hands, then wrap in clingfilm and chill for 30 minutes or so.

Roll out the dough to fit a 28cm/11 in tart tin, prick all over and chill well – preferably overnight.

Preheat the oven to 190°C/375°F/Gas 5.

Fill the pastry case with foil and baking beans, and bake blind in the preheated oven for 15 minutes. Remove the foil and cook for a further 5 minutes. Remove from the oven (leaving the oven on) and cool.

Beat together the filling ingredients (taste it if you can bear to, to ensure you have just enough seasoning, adding more chilli, salt and pepper if necessary).

Pour the filling into the pastry case and bake in the preheated oven for 40–45 minutes until the filling is set and tinged golden brown. Serve warm or cold.

These are perfect picnic fare – and are also great in lunch boxes. Should you have all day to fiddle in the kitchen, you can also make them with quails' eggs, which make dinky little canapés.

The herbs I like to use are a mixture of flat parsley and sage – but marjoram and thyme with parsley are also good.

Herby Scotch eggs

MAKES 12 halves

6 thick slices of wholemeal bread, processed into crumbs

600g/1 lb 5 oz quality sausage meat

2 heaped tablespoons porridge oats

3 heaped tablespoons freshly chopped herbs

salt and freshly ground black pepper

8 medium free-range eggs, (6 hard-boiled and shelled, plus 2, beaten)

1 level tablespoon plain flour, seasoned

oil, to deep-fry

Preheat the grill.

Toast the breadcrumbs for 4–5 minutes, turning often, until golden brown. Tip into a shallow bowl to cool.

Combine the sausage meat with the oats and herbs, then season generously with salt and pepper. (I find this easiest to do with my hands, not a spoon.) Divide into six.

Roll each hard-boiled egg in the flour, then, dipping your hands often in the flour, flatten out the sausage meat and mould it around each egg, ensuring each is evenly covered. Then coat each hard-boiled egg in the beaten egg, followed by the toasted crumbs. Place the eggs on a plate and refrigerate for at least 30 minutes.

Heat the oil to 180°C/350°F and, shaking occasionally, deep-fry the hard-boiled eggs in two batches for about 8 minutes each, until they look crunchy and deep golden brown.

Drain the eggs on kitchen paper and allow to cool, then cut in half to serve.

Wraps are handy for picnics, but should be prepared only shortly before leaving home – or made in situ. They can be made with myriad fillings, from hummus, tzatziki or guacamole to roasted peppers, salad, herbs or cheese. In the east of Turkey, I remember sitting around a table in the shade of the midday sun copying the locals as they prepared wraps with their wonderful 'village bread' (large rounds of flat bread), filled with sharp feta-style cheese, whole herb leaves (parsley, mint, basil), tomatoes and various salad leaves.

It is often easier to opt for self-assembly for these lovely kipper wraps since it can be a little messy – perfect for outdoor eating where finger-licking is positively encouraged.

Kipper pâté wraps

MAKES 4–6 wraps

4–6 soft flour tortillas
100g/3¹/₂ oz rocket

FOR THE PÂTÉ
2 large kippers or 300g/10¹/₂ oz
** kipper fillets, naturally cured**
25g/1 oz unsalted butter,
** softened**
50g/1³/₄ oz ricotta
juice of 1 lemon
a pinch of ground mace
salt and freshly ground black
** pepper**

For the pâté, place the kippers in a bowl or tall jug and cover with boiling water. Leave for about an hour, then drain well and pat dry. Peel off the skin and place the flesh, discarding as many bones as possible, in a food processor. Add the butter, ricotta, lemon juice and mace. Whiz until smooth, then add pepper to taste. You will probably not need any salt.

Spoon the mixture into a bowl and refrigerate until needed.

For the wraps, lay the tortillas out on a board. Spread a thick strip of kipper pâté over the bottom third of the tortilla, then top with rocket and season with a little pepper. Fold in the sides of the tortilla, then roll away from you. Trim the ends, and wrap in sandwich paper to take on your picnic.

In New England, where lobster rolls are popular during the summer, they are often made with hot dog or burger buns. I prefer good chewy sourdough or ciabatta rolls which have a better texture.

If you want to boil your own lobster (although most good fishmongers will boil to order), first pop it into the freezer for 2 hours before plunging it into a large pan of boiling salted water and, ensuring it is fully immersed, boil vigorously for 15–20 minutes, depending on its size.

Lobster mayo rolls

SERVES 4

cooked meat of 1 medium or large
   lobster, chopped into chunks
3 heaped tablespoons
   mayonnaise
chopped spring onion or dill
   or chervil, optional
salt and freshly ground black
   pepper
4 rolls (sourdough or ciabatta)

Mix the lobster with the mayonnaise and spring onion or herbs, if using, and season with salt and pepper to taste.

Fill the rolls with the mixture and squish down the tops. It is best to wrap the rolls in foil to take on the picnic.

This may not be a classic method of cooking salmon but, believe me, it works. Because of the heat of the machine and the fact that the fish is well wrapped in foil, the fish remains wonderfully moist and tasty. There are, however, various important things to remember, the first of which is that before you begin to cook the fish, run an empty cycle through the machine, to ensure it is as clean as possible. The second golden rule is to remember not to add any dishwasher powder to the machine before setting it off. That might sound terribly obvious but I can't tell you how tempting it is.

And, last but by no means least, don't forget to take on your picnic a good bottle of white wine in the cool box, alongside the King of Fish and the delicious watercress mayonnaise.

Dishwasher salmon with watercress mayo

SERVES 6–8

olive oil
1 salmon (about 1.8–2kg/
    4 lb–4 lb 8 oz gutted, cleaned
    weight), washed and dried
1 large unwaxed lemon, sliced
salt and freshly ground black
    pepper

FOR THE WATERCRESS MAYO
25g/1 oz watercress
4 tablespoons mayonnaise
2 tablespoons fromage frais
1 teaspoon horseradish sauce
salt and freshly ground black
    pepper

Having first prepared the dishwasher (see above), lay out a large sheet of foil and oil it, then lay the fish on top. Stuff the salmon with the lemon slices and season with salt and pepper. Wrap the fish in the foil, followed by two more sheets of foil. It is vital that there are no holes but if you do accidentally make a tear, patch it well.

Place the salmon on the top rack of the dishwasher: because of the spikes, I find it easier to place a wire cake rack on top of the spikes and lay the fish on that: it will slope, but at least it will not be impaled on the spikes. Turn the machine on to its longest, hottest cycle (mine is for glasses and heats the water to 65°C/150°F). It ought to last about 80–90 minutes. When the cycle is finished, leave the door shut for at least 20 minutes before carefully removing the fish and allowing it to cool in the foil.

Carefully place the salmon on a large sheet of clingfilm and wrap it, ready to take on your picnic.

For the mayo, whiz everything together in a food processor and season to taste with salt and pepper.

There are many variations of this deliciously moist picnic loaf. Because it is jam-packed with scrummy filling, it is seriously messy to eat, which makes it perfect for outdoors.

Although sun-dried tomatoes are rather – well – passé, they still impart a very special flavour to robust dishes such as this. If you cannot find sun-dried tomatoes in extra virgin olive oil, then do not use the oil from the jar: rather, use regular extra virgin oil.

Ciabatta picnic loaf with farmhouse cheese

For the cheese, I like to use any of the following Scottish farmhouse cheeses (all of which are classified as hard cheeses but are pliable enough to slice thinly with ease). Two cow's milk cheeses made with organic milk are Carola from Moray in the north of Scotland which is soft and delicately textured, and Criffel from Dumfriesshire, which has a tangy, floral taste. Bonnet, from Ayrshire, is my favourite hard goat's cheese and has a pleasantly mild flavour.

Remember to prepare the loaf on the eve of your picnic to give the flavours time to merge overnight in the fridge.

SERVES 6

1 ciabatta loaf

1 × 280g jar of sun-dried
tomatoes in extra virgin
olive oil

3 heaped tablespoons pesto
(red or green)

50g/1¾ oz rocket

1 extra large tomato, thinly sliced

salt and freshly ground black
pepper

100g/3½ oz quality salami,
thinly sliced

150g/5½ oz farmhouse cheese

Cut the loaf in half lengthways and remove about 2 tablespoons of the soft bread inside, to leave more room for the filling. Place both halves side by side on a board.

If you have been able to find sun-dried tomatoes in extra virgin oil, strain off 2 tablespoons oil from the jar; otherwise, use a regular extra virgin olive oil. Drizzle the oil over one half of the loaf, and spread the pesto over the other half. Pile the rocket on top of the pesto and squish down. Place the tomato slices on top and season to taste with salt and pepper.

Remove about half the sun-dried tomatoes from the jar, and chop roughly; then place on top of the tomato slices. Cover with the salami.

Remove the rind from the cheese then slice the cheese thinly and add to the pile. Place the other half of the ciabatta on the top and clamp the two halves together. Tuck in any bits of filling that are trying to escape. Tightly wrap the ciabatta in double foil, then in clingfilm. Place the parcel in the salad drawer of your fridge with a heavy weight, such as cartons of juice, on top. Next day, take the loaf to your picnic and cut it with a very sharp knife.

This is a sandwich, but not as most people know it …

What could be more homely and simple than a mustard-enhanced ham sandwich? But because most of us travel to picnics by car, this one also requires the diner to sit on the sandwich to help everything blend together, the butter melting seductively into the bread and the mustard and ham blissfully uniting. It is not simply a gimmick – although the kids love it when you ask them to sit on their lunch – it also tastes wonderful.

The idea for this sat-upon sandwich is from American food writer M.F.K Fisher's 'Railroad Sandwich' (from her 1976 book, The Art of Eating*) which her family perfected on long train journeys. They called upon a fellow passenger (in her words, 'a serene onlooker'), preferably one of ample girth, to do the sitting. Timing is not crucial but, depending on girth and corpulence, I advise a minimum of 20 minutes.*

Squashed ham sandwich

SERVES 2

**1 short, wide French loaf (about
    30cm/12 in long)**
55–75g/2 –2¾ oz butter
wholegrain or Dijon mustard
**about 115g/4 oz quality cooked
    ham, sliced**

Slice the loaf horizontally into 2 halves. Remove some of the soft bread inside to make more room for the filling. Spread both cut sides generously with the butter, then smear mustard on to one side.

Place the ham slices along one half, then top with the other half, pressing down firmly together. Never consider adding extras such as tomatoes or lettuce, unless you want a perfectly squashed sandwich with judiciously measured filling to end up a slimy disaster.

Wrap the loaf in foil, then in a plastic bag and finally in a tea towel. Ask the chosen sandwich-squasher to sit on the loaf (gently but firmly) for about 20–30 minutes.

Before eating, carefully unwrap the sandwich, cut in two and devour.

The ingredients for these sandwiches are flexible, depending how much smoked venison you can afford. If you are feeling extravagant, place the slices overlapping.

Cold-smoked venison is now fairly widely available and is a handy fridge standby, to serve as an impromptu starter with figs or slices of melon, or as part of an antipasti platter with good bread and olives.

These sandwiches are reminiscent of the reindeer sandwiches I often enjoyed during the year I lived in the north of Finland. There, any long journey, by train or car, was incomplete without an array of wonderful local fare from smoked reindeer on dark, sticky rye bread to sweet cardamom-flavoured buns called pulla *to go with the ubiquitous flasks of coffee.*

Smoked venison on rye

SERVES 1

thinly sliced rye bread
butter
horseradish sauce
smoked venison
rocket
salt and freshly ground black
   pepper

Lightly butter the slices of bread and lay out. Spread half the slices with a smear of horseradish, then top with venison. Pile on some rocket and season with salt and pepper, then top with the remaining bread. Cut in half and serve.

This is the most moist, moreish – and boozy – fruit cake imaginable. It is a far cry from those cakes that might look gorgeous but, once cut, are in fact disappointingly dry and crumbly. Because the fruit for this cake is soaked in whisky overnight, the fruit is plumped up and the flavour redolent of Scotland's national drink.

The cake keeps well – wrapped in foil and tucked away in an airtight tin – for two or three weeks. However, I can assure you that, should you take this on a picnic, it is extremely unlikely that you will bring any home.

Whisky-laced fruit cake

SERVES 12

250g/9 oz sultanas
250g/9 oz raisins
250g/9 oz currants
100g/3½ oz mixed peel
50g/1¾ oz glacé cherries
400ml/ 14 fl oz whisky
150g/5½ oz butter, softened
150g/5½ oz light muscovado sugar
3 large free-range eggs
200g/7 oz plain flour
1 teaspoon baking powder
2 teaspoons mixed spice
25g/1 oz ground almonds

Soak all the fruit in the whisky overnight. (If it is really warm – unlikely as that is in Scotland – I put it into the fridge overnight, then bring back to room temperature well before mixing.)

Preheat the oven to 170°C/325°F/Gas 3.

Butter a 22–23cm/8½–9 in, deep cake tin and line the sides of the tin with high lining paper which protects the surface from burning. You may need to cover the cake loosely with foil towards the end of cooking anyway.

Cream the butter and sugar together until soft and light. Add the eggs one by one, then tip in all the fruit (which will by now have absorbed all the whisky).

Sift in the flour, baking powder and mixed spice, and combine well.

Spoon the mixture into the prepared cake tin and bake the cake in the preheated oven for 1¾–2 hours or until done. Test this by inserting a skewer into the centre: it should come out clean. Remove the cake to a wire rack and leave in the tin until completely cold, then invert.

A beach bonfire

IT WAS EARLY JUNE 1989 and we had taken a short holiday on Islay with the children who were all quite small. Anticipating downpours and gales, we were well prepared, our kit including wellies, waterproofs and woolly jumpers, all of which are the norm on Scottish holidays. This one, however, was different. I still look back at those photographs and cannot believe we were not in Bermuda for we had landed on Islay in the midst of a heat wave.

Instead of lugging wind-breaks and macs down to the beach, we had to roll up trousers (we hadn't even brought shorts) and strip down to vests (this is Scotland; vests are not seasonal). It was absolutely stunning with desolate, white sandy beaches, our only company being the odd cow paddling along the shore to cool off. For once, our beach bonfire was not torture, huddling around a fire in an attempt to keep warm, having spent hours finding dry kindling. This was a dream – and the bonfire sausages, foil-wrapped bananas and marshmallows on sticks tasted all the better for it.

Fast forward a few years and our next Scottish west-coast holiday was to Lewis in the Outer Hebrides. The week started off fine but, by day three, not only did the July temperature never rise above 10°C, it also rained. Constantly. Undaunted, we battled on: we dragged equipment down to the beach (if the English are stoics, the Scots are worse) and huddled close to the fire which we had lit in the shelter of rocks and wind-breaks, the latter having taken for ever to erect in the blustery wind. Yet again, the bonfire sausages tasted wonderful, possibly even better as they were also providing inner warmth, our trusty thermals having failed to give us adequate protection.

Something like a happy medium would be pleasant for a good Scottish holiday, but I'm afraid the Lewis experience is more the norm. You can still have fun, however, provided you have efficient radiators at home to dry off wet clothes.

The recipes in this chapter are suitable for outdoor bonfires or for barbecues on your patio at home. Whichever you choose, remember to over-cater, for there is nothing more alluring than the smell of smoky food charring nicely over the embers of a fire – whether in a heat wave or in a Force 6 wind!

The simplicity of this dish belies its greatness. For what could be better than really good bread, toasted in front of a bonfire or on a barbecue, and smeared while hot with tomatoes and garlic, then topped with the best olive oil and a sprinkling of sea salt. At a bonfire, it is the prefect prelude to cooking your bangers, to assuage huge appetites that inevitably arise out of doors.

A few anchovy fillets can also be strewn on the toast at the last minute if you like.

Bonfire toast with tomatoes

SERVES 2

2 thick slices of country-style or
sourdough bread
1 ripe tomato, halved
1 fat garlic clove, peeled and
halved
extra virgin olive oil
sea salt

Lightly toast the bread on both sides until golden brown, not charred.

Rub the cut side of the tomato all over one side of the toast so the seeds remain on the toast. Quickly follow this by doing the same with the garlic. Drizzle with a little of the oil, then sprinkle with salt. Eat at once.

Dampers are scone-like bread, baked over a bonfire. A traditional Australian outback style of food, it needs little preparation, apart from mixing flour, water or milk, salt and sugar. Then you mould the prepared dough around the top end of green sticks which should be about 1 metre/3 feet long.

Dampers

The first task for my children on our family picnics is to collect wood for the fire, and suitable green sticks for the dampers and sausages; it is important to find green sticks still with the sap in them so they will burn less easily.

The main thing about cooking dampers is to do it slowly, otherwise you will bite into a burnt outside and a soft, uncooked doughy centre.

Once cooked, they can be used as dunkers into bowls of hummus (and are especially good with Fresh pea hummus, page 83), guacamole or salsa; or they can be smothered in butter and jam.

My younger daughter, Jessica, likes to stick a Peperami sausage down the centre and scoff it while it is piping hot.

MAKES 8–10

500g/1 lb 2 oz self-raising flour,
   sifted
1 heaped teaspoon salt
1 heaped teaspoon sugar
375–400ml/13–14 fl oz
   milk/water, mixed

Before you leave home, mix the flour, salt and sugar in a bowl, then mix in enough milk/water to form a soft but stiffish dough. (It should be soft enough to mould around your sticks, yet not too sticky so it is impossible to manage.)

Place the dough in a container with a tight lid, and take it in the cool box to the beach.

Once the flames of your bonfire have died down and you have nicely glowing embers, take off a piece of dough and wrap it around the end of the stick: mould it so the dough is about 2cm/¾ in all over. Or roll out the dough to form a long rope, then roll that around the stick to form a 'twister'.

Cook the dampers slowly over the embers for at least 15–20 minutes, turning gently to cook all sides. Twisters will probably take less time to cook.

Once they are a dark, golden brown, remove them from the stick. And now comes the fun. Dunk the dampers into a bowl of lovely fresh pea hummus (page 83) or smother them in butter, then dunk into jam, honey or maple syrup.

Although this Thai-inspired dipping sauce is wonderful with the langoustines, you could also mix some finely chopped lemon grass, root ginger and a little chopped chilli into some mayonnaise for a richer sauce.

Blanching the langoustines not only quickly kills them, it makes them easier to handle with tongs since they fold up nicely in the boiling water. Be sure to run them under cold water once blanched, however, to arrest the cooking.

If you are going to barbecue the langoustines on the beach, it is sensible to blanch them first at home, just before leaving. The sauce should be made in advance, too.

Barbecued langoustines with dipping sauce

SERVES 4

12–16 live langoustines

FOR THE DIPPING SAUCE

2 tablespoons molasses sugar

5 tablespoons white wine vinegar

1 tablespoon Thai fish sauce (nam pla)

1 tablespoon dark soy sauce

juice of 1 lime

½ red chilli, seeded and finely chopped

1 heaped tablespoon chopped fresh coriander

For the sauce, put the first 5 ingredients in a small pan and bring them slowly to the boil. When you see bubbles and the sugar is dissolved, remove the pan from the heat and pour the liquid into a bowl to cool. Then stir in the chilli and coriander.

Before barbecuing, first blanch the langoustines: plunge them into a pan of madly boiling water, bring the water back to the boil, then remove it immediately from the heat. Tip the langoustines into a colander and hold under the running cold tap.

Once dry, place the langoustines on the barbecue (no oil is required) and cook for about 4 minutes, turning.

To eat, shell and dip the delicious flesh into the sauce.

This is surely the best bonfire treat of all. A hot sausage on a stick eaten outside, with smoke billowing about as you perch over the embers, is quite simply unsurpassed for aroma, anticipation and taste. Then, once wrapped in a mustard-smeared soft tortilla (or bread roll, if you prefer), it matters not a jot that the greasy juices dribble over your shoes or on to the beach as you bite into your sausage, for that is the joy of outdoor eating where Messy is synonymous with Good.

Bonfire sausages under wraps

SERVES 4–6

8–12 quality sausages (fat not skinny)
8–12 soft wheat tortillas
Dijon mustard

Spear the sausages on green sticks and roast over the glowing embers of the bonfire until cooked. This can take up to 15 minutes, depending on the heat of the fire. Remember, the sausage can look ready – all nicely charred outside – but still be completely raw inside, so cook thoroughly.

Meanwhile, spread the tortillas with mustard. When the sausages are cooked, wrap each one in the middle of a tortilla, roll up and devour.

This is a delicious – if messy – sandwich: a juicy barbecued steak clamped between a lovely mustard- and mayo-lined chewy roll. It does, in fact, make the eating easier if you neatly slice the beef before placing it in the roll, but maybe that seems a little too cheffy.

The choice of steak is up to you: sirloin or rib-eye are great on flavour but rump also tastes superb and is less expensive.

As for your choice of bread, ciabatta, sourdough or proper baguette are good but think about the size of the steak and how it will fit in: the bread should be long rather than round, so a wide baguette, cut in half to accommodate two steaks, is ideal.

Barbecued steak sandwich

SERVES 2

2 long ciabatta or sourdough rolls, or 1 wide baguette (cut in two)
mayonnaise
Dijon mustard
lettuce
salt and freshly ground black pepper
2 steaks, trimmed

Open out the rolls or the baguette halves, and spread one half with mayonnaise and the other with mustard. Strew lettuce on the mayonnaise half.

Season the steaks with salt and pepper and barbecue until cooked to your liking: I reckon on 2–2$\frac{1}{2}$ minutes on each side for medium-rare. Place directly on to the lettuce, clamp down the lid and devour messily.

The principle of cooking a whole chicken over a beer can is similar to thrusting halved lemons or onions inside a chicken as it roasts: to impart moisture. The beer can also ensures that the chicken can stand upright and so the beery vapours impregnate the entire bird, leaving it fabulously moist inside, yet nicely charred and barbecued outside.

This method of cooking is also a great talking point at your barbecue and, indeed, many cans of beer are likely to be consumed as the beery aroma tempts eager diners as they stand around waiting for the chicken to cook.

Only make this dish if you have a barbecue with a lid. And note the can size – small rather than the regular size.

Beer can chicken

SERVES 6

1.2–1.3kg (2 lb 11 oz–3 lb) free-range chicken

olive oil

coarse sea salt and freshly ground black pepper

1 × 330ml can of beer, wiped and dried

First rub the chicken all over with oil, then season with salt and pepper.

Now open the beer and take a few gulps – the can needs to be around half full. Place the can on a solid surface. Holding a chicken leg in each hand, thrust the cavity over the can so it is firmly stuck.

Carefully transfer the can and chicken to the barbecue and place it in the middle of the grill, using the chicken's legs to balance it like a tripod. Do not move it from now until the end of cooking.

Cover the chicken with the barbecue's lid and cook over a medium or medium-low heat for about 1 hour. Test it is ready by piercing the thigh: the juices should run clear.

When it is ready, remove the chicken very carefully (don't forget the can will contain boiling beer). Gently take the chicken off the can and leave it to rest on a serving dish for 10 minutes before carving.

This is a wonderful dish not only because the chicken tastes good but also because it means you have a little appetiser thrown in. The spice mix is based on the Egyptian dukkah – a mixture of nuts and spices, roasted and then crushed, and eaten with bread dipped in olive oil. In Egypt, it is served for breakfast or as an appetiser.

I suggest you set out a little dish of the mixture with some cubes of good bread and a dish of olive oil. Invite your guests to dip the bread into the oil and then dunk it into the spice mix. It is absolutely delicious with drinks, as the aroma of the chicken rises temptingly from the barbecue.

Spice-rubbed barbecued chicken

SERVES 6–8

16–20 chicken drumsticks
    or 2 chickens, jointed

FOR THE SPICE MIX
75g/2¾ oz sesame seeds
25g/1 oz cumin seeds
25g/1 oz coriander seeds
50g/1¾ oz hazelnuts, roughly
    chopped
salt and freshly ground black
    pepper

For the spice mix, place everything except the seasoning in a frying pan and dry-fry (without fat) for 3–4 minutes or until a lovely spice aroma arises. Shake the pan frequently.

Tip the roasted spices and nuts into a spice mill or small electric blender and blitz briefly (using the pulse button) until the spices are crushed but still dry; they should not be oily. Season with salt and pepper to taste.

Tip about three-quarters of the spice mix into a large plastic bag and add the chicken pieces. Toss the bag about until the chicken pieces are well coated, then leave for several hours in the fridge.

When ready to cook, place the chicken on the barbecue and cook for about 25 minutes or until the joints are cooked through.

Unsophisticated and simple, this dish is a throwback to the days when, as Girl Guides, we sat around a camp fire, singing and cooking sausages in the embers. The grand finale, when the fire was almost out, was to bury chocolate-studded bananas wrapped in foil, and keep them there until the bananas were piping hot and gooey. There is really no better taste from a beach bonfire.

Do be sure to wait a little before devouring the banana or you will – as many Girl Guides have done before – burn your tongue on the hot chocolate.

Chocolate bananas in foil

SERVES 4

4 large bananas
1 bar quality milk or plain chocolate, in squares

Split the (unpeeled) bananas lengthways with a sharp knife and tuck some chocolate down the middle. Wrap each banana in foil and cook them in the embers (or on the rack over your barbecue) for about 10–15 minutes, depending on the heat of your fire. Test by peeking inside one of the foil parcels; they are ready when the chocolate is molten and gooey.

Remove the foil parcels with tongs and open carefully.

This is an American camp-fire treat ... a sandwich of digestive biscuits (graham crackers in the US), marshmallows and chocolate. It is such a nostalgia-invoking treat in the States that it is cropping up on their sophisticated restaurant dessert menus, with home-made biscuits, marshmallows and a bitter chocolate ganache. To my mind, this rather misses the point, which is the gooey marshmallow and chocolate intermingling between hot biscuits and being devoured out of doors while sitting around the last of the bonfire embers.

Mini marshmallows are best for this, but if only large ones are available, each can be cut into half for the s'mores. You can also cook them whole speared on a stick and held over the fire until soft. Do not do this if you have bare feet since the melted marshmallows easily drop off the stick and if they drop on to your toes, as I know from bitter experience, you will discover how a duck with webbed feet feels.

S'mores

SERVES 4

8 digestive biscuits
1 packet of mini marshmallows
**1 bar of quality milk or plain
   chocolate, in squares**

Place 4 biscuits on a board and top with the marshmallows and chocolate. Place another biscuit on top of each and wrap in foil.

Place the foil packages in the embers (or on the rack over the barbecue coals) for 5–10 minutes, depending on the heat of the fire. Remove them with tongs and carefully unwrap.

Hogmanay

I CAN REMEMBER at Hogmanay feeling like Liesl in *The Sound of Music.* You remember the scene where she begs the Captain for her first sip of champagne. I didn't have the gorgeous white dress (more likely I was wearing thick woollens and hiking boots, ready for First Footing), but somehow I felt that pang of being hard done by as I watched everyone else sipping 'proper' drinks while I was only ever allowed lemonade. Until one year when I was allowed an advocaat and lemonade. Oh, the joy of tasting that first Snowball! Nowadays, the very thought of it is repugnant, but the thick, sweet drink was nectar to my then untuned palate.

As I grew up, Hogmanay – or New Year's Eve – was always a time for friends and fun. Friends and neighbours would get together to have a drink and the traditional shortbread (often eaten with cheese), sultana cake, black bun and such delights as ginger or blackcurrant cordial – Scotland's answer to champagne, I suppose. The jollities would continue until 'The Bells' and then the proper partying would begin. It was one of the few times of year Scots kissed each other in public: I remember having to endure pecks on the cheek by bristly bearded first footers while wishing everyone a Happy New Year.

First Footing had its own rituals, for traditionally it was a dark man who was first over the doorstep, bearing a piece of coal for luck. Then, once the first footers had begun their rounds, they were on a roll, not stopping until every house with lights on was visited and the New Year toasted yet again. It was all great fun, especially during the not infrequently snowy or icy Hogmanays when tramping around on foot became highly dangerous and yet somehow hilarious (this was some years after that first Snowball). But it did not stop there. Even when you had gone to bed – in the 'wee small hours' – there was the prospect of it happening all over again, for First Footing continued with a vengeance later that day. Whereas Hogmanay was all about friends, New Year's Day was all about family, when duty visits were obligatory, hangovers or not.

Nowadays, there is rather more emphasis on food, with many people having friends for dinner. However, after midnight strikes, they continue to party the night away. So, little change there then.

These bannocks are lovely soft, thick cakes made of oatmeal and flour. They differ from oatcakes which are thinner and more crispy. They are wonderful served warm with the Scallop ceviche (see page 123) or with a bowl of hearty soup.

A girdle is traditional for making bannocks; you can use a large, heavy frying pan but it is rather more difficult to flip the bannocks unless you use a bendy spatula which can push down the sides of the frying pan.

If you cannot find buttermilk, you can use sour milk made by adding 1 teaspoon lemon juice to regular milk and leaving it to stand for 5 minutes.

Oatmeal bannocks

MAKES 4 large bannocks

175g/6 oz plain flour, sifted
200g/7 oz medium oatmeal
1 teaspoon salt
25g/1 oz butter
1 rounded teaspoon honey
1 teaspoon bicarbonate of soda
1½ teaspoons cream of tartar
250ml/9 fl oz buttermilk or sour milk

Mix the flour, oatmeal and salt in a bowl.

Over a gentle heat, melt the butter and honey.

Stir the bicarbonate of soda and cream of tartar into the milk, then tip this, together with the melted butter mixture, into the flour. Stir to combine.

Meanwhile, lightly butter a girdle (griddle) and heat over a medium heat until hot. Tip the mixture on to the girdle and spread out to form a circle, about 25cm/10 in diameter.

Leave to cook for about 5–6 minutes until the underside is set, then cut with a knife into quarters. Now carefully flip the quarters over. Lower the heat to medium-low and continue to cook until done – about another 7–8 minutes.

Remove the bannocks to a wire rack to cool slightly. Serve warm, split and spread with butter.

If you make the pancakes a couple of days in advance, wrap them in clingfilm and store them in the fridge. When you come to use them, wrap them in foil and reheat them in a low oven. If you make them on the day of serving, however, they need no reheating and can be served just as they are.

Make this size (dessertspoon) for canapés or use a tablespoon to make larger pancakes to serve on plates as a first course.

Smoked salmon is a good substitute if you cannot find the cold-smoked trout.

Scotch pancakes with smoked trout and sour cream

SERVES 8 (24–30 pancakes)

125g/4½ oz self-raising flour, sifted

100g/3½ oz wholemeal self-raising flour

2 large free-range eggs

300ml/½ pint milk

a pinch of salt

2 heaped teaspoons horseradish sauce

butter, for greasing

1 × 284ml tub soured cream

freshly ground black pepper

1 × 400g pack of cold-smoked trout

snipped chives or dill fronds, to garnish

Place the flours, eggs, milk and salt in a food processor, add 1 teaspoon of the horseradish sauce and process until smooth. (Or whisk by hand with a balloon whisk.)

Place a large, heavy-based frying pan or girdle (griddle) on a medium heat and lightly butter the surface, using kitchen paper. When the pan is sufficiently hot (test by dropping a teaspoonful of batter on to the surface: it should bubble within 1 minute), drop 1 dessertspoonful of batter into the pan and repeat three times to make 4 pancakes. After 1–2 minutes, you will see bubbles: this is the sign to flip the pancakes over. Cook for a further minute or so, until batter does not ooze out when lightly pressed with your fingers.

Remove to a wire rack and cover loosely with a tea towel. Continue making the pancakes until the batter is all used up.

For the topping, mix the soured cream with the remaining horseradish and some salt and pepper.

To serve, spoon some of the cream mixture over each pancake and garnish with some smoked trout and chives or dill.

Ceviche – made from all sorts of fish such as cod, haddock, swordfish, tuna (or red snapper in the coastal towns of Mexico where it is very popular) – can also be made with such delectable seafood as scallops. Ordinarily, you can serve this fresh-tasting dish with blue corn chips and perhaps a bowl of guacamole on the side, but we are in Scotland and so hearty oatmeal bannocks, warm – straight from the girdle – are what is required. Absolutely divine.

Scallop ceviche

SERVES 4

6 large fresh scallops

3 tablespoons freshly squeezed
   lime juice (approx. 3 small
   or 2 medium limes)

3–4 small vine-ripened tomatoes,
   diced

4 spring onions, finely chopped

2 heaped teaspoons freshly
   grated ginger

2 heaped tablespoons freshly
   chopped coriander

1 tablespoon olive oil

salt and freshly ground black
   pepper

salad leaves, to serve

Slice each scallop thinly into about 4 pieces (remove the orange coral if you prefer). Place the slices in a non-metallic bowl with 2 tablespoons of the lime juice. Stir gently and leave to marinate for 25–30 minutes at room temperature.

In a separate bowl, combine the tomatoes, spring onions, ginger, coriander, olive oil and the remaining lime juice with plenty of salt and pepper.

Drain off the liquid from the scallops and discard. Add the scallops to the tomato mixture and turn gently, taking care not to break them up. Arrange a bed of salad leaves on a shallow dish, then tip the scallop mixture on top. Serve within the hour, at room temperature, with the warm bannocks (see page 121).

This is a lovely hearty stew that is wonderful for informal entertaining, since the pan of goodies sits on the table and you decant straight from there into warm bowls. Then large chunks of good bread (I prefer sourdough) are dunked in with gay abandon. If the squid are fairly small, leave the tentacles whole.

Seafood stew with squid, mussels and tomatoes

SERVES 4

450g/1 lb fresh mussels

3 tablespoons olive oil

1 large onion, peeled and finely chopped

3 sticks of celery, finely chopped

3 garlic cloves, peeled and finely chopped

2 × 400g cans of chopped tomatoes in juice

400ml/14 fl oz red wine

1 tablespoon red wine or sherry vinegar

2 sprigs of rosemary

2 bay leaves

a small pinch of ground cinnamon

salt and freshly ground black pepper

about 300g/10½ oz squid, cleaned and sliced thickly

450g/1 lb cod or monkfish, cut into thick chunks

1 heaped tablespoon chopped flat parsley

Scrub the mussels well, discarding any open ones that don't close when tapped on a work surface.

Heat 2 tablespoons of the oil in a large casserole and gently fry the onion, celery and garlic for about 10 minutes, then add the tomatoes including the juice, 250ml/9 fl oz of the wine, the vinegar, rosemary sprigs, bay leaves and cinnamon and season with plenty of salt and pepper.

Bring to the boil, then lower the heat and simmer for about 20 minutes, uncovered, until the liquid has slightly thickened; stir once.

While the sauce is bubbling away, heat the remaining oil in a frying pan and, once hot, add the squid. Fry quickly for a couple of minutes until just cooked but still tender. Remove to a plate.

Add the remaining red wine to the casserole after the 20 minutes and bring to the boil. When the sauce is boiling, add the mussels, cover and cook for 2 minutes, then add the cod or monkfish. Cover and cook gently for 5–8 minutes or until the mussels are all opened and the fish just cooked. Discard any mussels that have not opened. Tip the squid into the pan and reheat gently. Check the seasoning, remove the rosemary and bay leaves, and then scatter over the parsley.

Serve straight from the casserole into warm bowls with plenty of good bread.

This is a delicious if rather unusual way to serve that glorious fish, halibut. I love the freshness of the garlicky, minty tzatziki with the oven-baked halibut.

You can get ahead by making the tzatziki in advance, then about an hour or so before serving, remove it from the fridge to allow it to come to room temperature. Do make it with real Greek yoghurt rather than Greek-style yoghurt.

Serve with warmed pitta bread or tiny boiled potatoes.

Halibut with tzatziki

SERVES 4

4 large thick fillets of halibut, skinned (each about 225g/8 oz)
salt and freshly ground black pepper
100ml/3¹/₂ fl oz dry white wine
25g/1 oz butter
sprigs of mint, to garnish

FOR THE TZATZIKI
1 medium cucumber, wiped
2 teaspoons salt
200ml/7 fl oz Greek yoghurt
1 tablespoon extra virgin olive oil
juice of ¹/₂ lemon
2 heaped tablespoons freshly chopped mint
2 garlic cloves, peeled and crushed
freshly ground black pepper

For the tzatziki, chop the ends off the cucumber then grate it – unpeeled – and place the grated flesh in a colander over a bowl. Sprinkle with the salt and leave for about an hour.

Preheat the oven to 220°C/425°F/Gas 7 and butter a shallow ovenproof dish.

Using your hands, squeeze out all the liquid from the cucumber, then pat it dry with paper towels. Place the cucumber in a bowl with the remaining ingredients and stir to combine.

Place the halibut fillets in the prepared dish. Season with salt and pepper, then pour over the wine.

Dot with the butter, then cook in the preheated oven for 12–15 minutes, depending on the thickness of the fish, until cooked through: you can check with the tip of a sharp knife.

To serve, place a mound of tzatziki on each warmed plate, top with the fish, and garnish with a sprig of mint.

We are fortunate to have some wonderful free-range chickens farmed in the Borders of Scotland. Linda Dick's chickens, in particular, are so good that whenever they are served at a dinner, everyone present wants to know where they can buy one. Her farm – Hamildean Farm near Peebles – has only about 50 birds at one time and they are the epitome of free-range. Killed aged between 12 and 14 weeks, the birds are dry-plucked and hung for up to a week, which gives them the most superb, lingering flavour and firm texture.

Roast Borders chicken with salsa verde

SERVES 8–10

4kg/9 lb chicken (or small turkey)
4 large unwaxed lemons
4 tablespoons extra virgin olive oil
sea salt and freshly ground black
**   pepper**

FOR THE SALSA VERDE
100g/3½ oz flat parsley
60g/2¼ oz mint
4 heaped tablespoons capers
4 heaped teaspoons Dijon mustard
3 fat garlic cloves, peeled and
**   chopped**
1 × 50g can of anchovies, drained
**   and snipped**
juice of 1 large lemon
6 tablespoons extra virgin olive oil

For the salsa verde, remove the leaves from the herbs, reserving the stalks. Place the leaves in a food processor. Add the capers, mustard, garlic, anchovies and lemon juice and whiz until blended; then add the olive oil and season with salt and pepper to taste.

Preheat the oven to 200°C/400°F/Gas 6. Set the chicken in a large, oiled baking tin and stuff with the reserved herb stalks. Quarter 2 of the lemons and tuck these inside too.

Grate the zest of the third lemon. Mix this, together with its juice, with the olive oil. Pour this slowly over the bird, season all over with salt and pepper, and make a loose foil tent to cover the chicken.

Roast the chicken in the preheated oven for 20 minutes, then reduce the oven temperature to 180°C/350°F/Gas 4 and cook for a further 20 minutes per 450g/1 lb, basting a couple of times.

About 40 minutes before the end of cooking, squeeze the fourth lemon and pour the juice over the chicken, baste well, then return it to the oven without the foil, to brown. Baste frequently.

Once cooked (test by inserting a skewer in the thickest part of the thigh: the juices should run clear), remove from the oven and allow to rest for 15–20 minutes. Drain off the pan juices and keep warm; taste and season. To serve, carve the chicken, pour over a little of the lemony pan juices and serve with a dollop of salsa verde on the side.

The lamb season begins later in Scotland than, say, the south of England, and we tend to have new-season lamb as a treat from May or June onwards, instead of March or April down south. Some hill lamb and lamb from the islands is even later. My butcher, Crombie's of Edinburgh, has Shetland lamb every year in the autumn, from lambs that have been born in the summer and then killed from late September until Christmas. If you can get it, Shetland lamb is a rare treat, with its distinctive flavour probably being enhanced from the seaweed that is part of their daily diet.

Serve this with couscous and a simple green salad dressed with a minty vinaigrette and thinly sliced, pared orange slices.

Slow-cooked lamb with chermoula

SERVES 6–8

1 large leg of lamb (about 2kg/4½ lb)

3 large onions, peeled and sliced
   into rings

½ teaspoon salt

1 teaspoon golden granulated
   sugar

FOR THE CHERMOULA

1 onion, peeled and chopped

6 garlic cloves, peeled and chopped

4 heaped tablespoons fresh
   coriander

3 heaped tablespoons flat parsley

2 tablespoons ground paprika

2 tablespoons ground cumin

2 teaspoons cayenne pepper

juice of 1 large lemon

3 tablespoons olive oil

1 teaspoon salt

For the chermoula, place all the ingredients in a food processor and process until blended.

Place the lamb in a non-metallic dish and prick all over with a fine skewer. Spread over the chermoula, trying to cover everywhere. Cover loosely with foil and refrigerate for 24–36 hours.

On the day of cooking, remove the lamb from the refrigerator 30 minutes or so before cooking.

Preheat the oven to 170°C/325°F/Gas 3.

Place the onion rings in the base of a roasting tin. Using your hands, toss them in the salt and sugar. Pour over 600ml/1 pint cold water. Place the lamb on top. Cook in the preheated oven for about 4 hours, basting every hour.

After cooking is completed, allow the joint to rest for 10–15 minutes, then serve slices of lamb with spoonfuls of the pan juices and the onions.

Although this is perfect served in the summer when Scottish raspberries are in season, it is also good during the dark winter months, using frozen raspberries. When I go berry-picking at my local pick-your-own farm, I always buy masses extra, then, once jam is made and tummies replete from over-indulging in the freshly picked fruit, the rest are frozen for winter.

Raspberry and Drambuie crème fraîche tart

SERVES 6

50g/1¾ oz and 3 tablespoons
    golden caster sugar
125g/4½ oz ground almonds
125g/4½ oz plain flour, sifted
125g/4½ oz butter, diced
1 medium and 2 large free-range
    eggs
1 × 200ml tub of crème fraîche,
    plus 4 heaped tablespoons
    to serve
4 tablespoons Drambuie
250g/9 oz raspberries

For the pastry, place the 50g/1¾ oz sugar, the almonds, flour and butter in a food processor, and process until it resembles breadcrumbs. Add the medium egg, and process. Gather the mixture into a ball, wrap in clingfilm and chill for 1 hour.

Roll out the dough to fit a 23cm/9 in deep tart tin. Prick the base, then chill for several hours, preferably overnight.

Preheat the oven to 190°C/375°F/Gas 5.

Line the pastry case with foil and baking beans and bake in the preheated oven for 15 minutes. Remove the foil and beans and cook for a further 10 minutes. Remove the pastry case from the oven (leaving the oven on) and allow to cool.

Beat together the remaining sugar, the 2 large eggs, the 200ml of crème fraîche and 2 tablespoons of the Drambuie. Pour the mixture into the pastry case. Arrange the raspberries in a single layer on top.

Bake in the preheated oven for 35 minutes or until just set. Allow to cool in the tin.

Beat the remaining crème fraîche with the remaining Drambuie and serve with the tart.

This is a delicious pudding that is both comforting and unusual, with the golden-yellow polenta crumble topping in place of the more common all-flour one. The butterscotch either comes from a jar in the form of dulce de leche, *that glorious (to sweet-toothed Scots, anyway) toffee from Argentina, or you can boil an unopened can of condensed milk for a couple of hours.*

Pear, almond and butterscotch crumble

SERVES 6

1kg/2¼ lb ripe pears
juice of 1 large lemon
75g/2¾ oz toasted flaked almonds
4 heaped tablespoons *dulce de leche*

FOR THE CRUMBLE TOPPING
100g/3½ oz polenta
100g/3½ oz plain flour
75g/2¾ oz golden caster sugar
90g/3¼ oz butter, diced
a pinch of salt

Preheat the oven to 180°C/350°F/Gas 4.

Peel and slice the pears. Place them in an ovenproof dish with the lemon juice. Toss gently to coat in the juice.

Top the pears with the almonds, then spoon over the *dulce de leche*, trying to cover all the pears and almonds.

For the crumble topping, combine the polenta, flour and sugar in a bowl, then rub in 75g/2¾ oz of the butter and salt. Tip this over the pear mixture and press down lightly.

Dot with the remaining butter and bake in the preheated oven for 35–40 minutes or until golden brown.

Allow the crumble to stand for about 10 minutes, then serve with Greek yoghurt or ice cream. Or both.

This is a lovely and very simple recipe that keeps well in an airtight container. It can also be used in the shortbread ice cream recipe on page 169.

Double choc chunk shortbread

MAKES 24 pieces

280g/10 oz unsalted butter, softened

175g/6 oz golden caster sugar

175g/6 oz quality chocolate (half milk, half dark), chopped into chunks

225g/8 oz plain flour, sifted

115g/4 oz semolina

a pinch of salt

Preheat the oven to 150°C/300°F/Gas 2 and butter a 23 × 33cm/ 9 × 13 in Swiss-roll tin.

Place the softened butter and sugar in a bowl. Using an electric hand-held mixer (on the lowest speed), beat together until light and fluffy.

Add the chocolate chunks, flour, semolina and salt; then, using a wooden spoon, stir gently to combine. Do not overbeat or stir too hard at this stage, or the shortbread will be tough. You should end up with a slightly crumbly mixture.

Turn the mixture into the prepared Swiss-roll tin. Dip the palm of your hand in flour and lightly pat the mixture down, pressing into the tin. Prick lightly all over with a fork.

Bake in the preheated oven for about 40 minutes or until pale golden brown.

Remove from the oven and, while the shortbread is still hot, cut it into squares or fingers, then leave it in the tin to cool. Transfer to a wire rack to cool completely.

Ne'er day

CHILDHOOD MEMORIES of Ne'er Day involve a car journey to Dundee to visit both sets of grandparents and an embarrassment of aunts, uncles and cousins. Many of these journeys seemed to involve snow for, although I can only remember one genuinely white Christmas as a child, New Year was not only often bitterly cold but snowy or, at least, very frosty.

After the long (or so it seemed then) journey from Edinburgh and through Fife, there would be at least six stops all over Dundee to have the obligatory New Year drink and a dip into all those Party Susans (tupperware platters divided into sections), overflowing with cubes of cheese, crisps and pickled onions. At my great-auntie Maggie's flat, up three flights of stairs, there was blackcurrant cordial and 'shortie', with whisky on offer, of course, for the men and the sweetest of sweet sherry for the ladies. The New Year's Day meal was – certainly in Dundee – always steak pie which was a delicious, meaty, gravy-enriched stew with a flaky topping, served with mashed potatoes and either a green vegetable such as cabbage or, more likely in Dundee, some other accompaniment such as butter beans. Utterly delicious, as I recall.

My sister's family, who live in Arbroath, north of Dundee, continue to celebrate Ne'er Day in the old-fashioned way with local parties only beginning on 2 January and going on sometimes for two or three days. We Scots might be considered frugal, but never where fun is concerned.

Although the perspective on Hogmanay has changed a little over the years, with food being given slightly more emphasis (more and more people going out to dinner first), New Year's Day has remained pretty much unchanged, with delicious food (still often steak pie) that is easy to prepare in advance since there are still sore heads – even after a food-filled Hogmanay.

Once the New Year's Day meal is over, the First Footing continues for a few more days. And with 'street parties' in all the major Scottish cities these days, Ne'er Day is still a time for families to get together and celebrate in the time-honoured manner, with tradition very much to the fore – although, thankfully, I have not seen Party Susans around for quite some time.

These are delicious canapés, equally suited to precede a meat or fish dinner. The confit is rich and sweetish, and the cheese, with its mild goatiness, complements it perfectly. If Ayrshire-produced Bonnet isn't available, use another hard, mildish goat's cheese.

Crostini with Bonnet goat's cheese and onion confit

MAKES about 20

1 long, thin french stick (ficelle) or Italian sfilatino, cut into rounds
olive oil
about 50g/1¾ oz Bonnet, shaved

FOR THE ONION CONFIT
75g/2¾ oz butter
2 large onions, peeled and sliced thinly
4 tablespoons dry vermouth or white wine
2 tablespoons honey
4 tablespoons sherry vinegar
salt and freshly ground black pepper

For the confit, melt the butter, then gently cook the onions until they are softened – about 15 minutes, stirring.

Add the vermouth or wine, honey and vinegar, season with salt and pepper, and stir well. Cook gently for 20–30 minutes, stirring often, until the mixture has thickened. Check the seasoning and allow to cool.

Meanwhile, preheat the oven to 180°C/350°F/Gas 4.

Place the bread rounds on a baking sheet and lightly brush the tops with oil. Bake in the preheated oven for 10–15 minutes or until pale golden. Allow to cool.

Just before serving, spread some confit on to a crostini and top it with a sliver of goat's cheese. Serve at once.

I like to use a fresh, firm goat's cheese such as Bonnet for this; Ticklemore from Devon is also good. The cheese should not be as strong as, say, a Crottin de Chavignol, which would totally overpower the salmon, but should have a pleasingly goaty taste.

Serve with tiny boiled new potatoes and stir-fried Savoy cabbage, kale or pak choi.

Roast salmon with goat's cheese

SERVES 4

4 salmon escalopes
   (or middle-cut fillets), skinned
olive oil
salt and freshly ground black
   pepper
4 thin slices of goat's cheese

Preheat the oven to 220°C/425°F/Gas 7.

Place the salmon on a lightly oiled baking sheet and season well with salt and pepper.

Cook in the preheated oven for 5 minutes, then remove. Place a slice of cheese on top of each piece of salmon, then return to the oven for a further 2–3 minutes, depending on the thickness of the salmon, until just done.

Serve on warm plates.

The trick in keeping the pheasant moist when roasting is to roast it quickly, basting often, then allowing it to rest. The skirlie can be made in advance, then loosely covered in foil and reheated in a medium oven for about 10 minutes until it is piping hot. Medium oatmeal is most commonly used for the skirlie but I like half medium and half pinhead for a nicely nutty texture. Make sure frozen blackcurrants are thoroughly defrosted.

Although one medium to large pheasant will ordinarily only serve 3 (generously) or 4 (provided you are also offering a starter and/or pudding), the quantities for the sauce and skirlie in the recipe below are enough for 2 pheasants to serve 6–8 people.

Pheasant with skirlie and blackcurrants

SERVES 4

1 tablespoon olive oil

25g/1 oz butter

1 oven-ready pheasant (weighing
    about 1.25–1.3kg/2³⁄₄ lb–3 lb)

salt and freshly ground black
    pepper

100ml/3¹⁄₂ fl oz gin

1 × 200ml tub of crème fraîche

2 tablespoons blackcurrant jelly

200g/7 oz blackcurrants

FOR THE SKIRLIE

50g/1³⁄₄ oz dripping (or 25g/
    1 oz butter and 2 tablespoons
    olive oil)

1 medium onion, peeled and very
    finely chopped

100g/3¹⁄₂ oz oatmeal

Preheat the oven to 200°C/400°F/Gas 6.

For the pheasant, heat the oil and butter in a roasting tin and brown the bird all over (which can take up to 5 minutes). Baste well with the fat, then season with salt and pepper. Place in the preheated oven for about 45 minutes or until done, basting 2–3 times as it roasts.

While the pheasant is cooking, make the skirlie. Heat the fat in a frying pan, then add the onion and cook slowly for about 10 minutes until softened. Add the oatmeal, stirring until the fat is absorbed. Cook over a medium heat for about 10 minutes or until toasted and crumbly. Season to taste with salt and pepper.

Test whether the pheasant is cooked by piercing the meat near the thigh and leg joint: the juices should be a very pale pink (not reddish pink). Remove the bird to a carving dish and keep warm, loosely covered with foil. Allow to rest for at least 10 minutes.

Place the roasting tin on a direct flame, then add the gin – carefully if you are cooking over a naked flame. Let the juices bubble away for 3–4 minutes, scraping the bottom of the pan to ensure all the bits are included, then add the crème fraîche and blackcurrant jelly. Stirring well, cook gently for 4–5 minutes until the sauce has thickened slightly. Add the blackcurrants and salt and pepper to taste, heat for a further couple of minutes until it is all piping hot. Check the seasoning again.

Carve the pheasant and serve with some sauce and a mound of skirlie.

I recommend serving this with the neep and olive oil mash which follows, or a mound of pappardelle; a creamy potato gratin is also good.

Neeps, also known as turnips in Scotland (swedes to southerners), are one of Scotland's favourite vegetables. Usually served boiled and mashed with butter, it is the perfect accompaniment to game, beef, pork, haggis – or good old mince. This version is by no means traditional but is extremely delicious, nonetheless. Be sure to be generous with the freshly ground pepper.

Neep and olive oil mash

SERVES 4–6

700–750g/1 lb 9 oz–1 lb 10 oz neeps
about 350g/12 oz potatoes
salt and freshly ground black pepper
about 3 tablespoons extra virgin olive oil

Peel the neeps and potatoes and cut into large chunks. Cook them in boiling salted water for about 20 minutes, or until tender; then drain. Return the vegetables to the pan and, over the heat, let them dry out completely, shaking the pan often.

Once the vegetables are dry, mash them with a potato masher, then gradually add the oil. You might find you need a little more oil to make a smooth, rich mash. Season to taste with salt and plenty of pepper, and serve at once.

Roast rib of beef is such a treat – and utterly delicious. It is also very versatile, going well with myriad accompaniments from traditional Yorkshire puddings, roast potatoes, gravy and horseradish sauce to sauté potatoes, a mound of soft polenta or – my favourite – a thyme-flavoured barley risotto. And, as here, a creamy, wild mushroom sauce.

Roast beef with wild mushroom sauce

SERVES 8

4-bone rib of beef (about 4.25kg/9½ lb)

salt and freshly ground black pepper

2 × 10g packs dried porcini

500ml/18 fl oz dry white wine

450g/1 lb fresh mushrooms, preferably chestnut or shiitake

75g/2¾ oz butter

1 tablespoon olive oil

4 garlic cloves, peeled and chopped

25g/1 oz plain flour

225ml/8 fl oz double cream

Allow the beef to come to room temperature for an hour or so before cooking.

Preheat the oven to 230°C/450°F/Gas 8.

Season the beef all over with salt and pepper, then place in a large roasting tin and roast (without any extra fat) in the preheated oven for 15 minutes. Then reduce the oven temperature to 170°C/325°F/Gas 3 and continue to roast for a further 17 minutes per 450g/1 lb plus 15 minutes. This will produce medium-rare meat and you should adjust the cooking time if you prefer very rare or well-done meat.

While the meat is cooking, prepare the sauce. Rinse the porcini and soak them in the wine for about 30 minutes. Wipe and roughly chop the fresh mushrooms.

Melt the butter and olive oil in a large saucepan and gently fry the garlic for about 1 minute, then add the fresh mushrooms. Drain the soaking porcini, reserving the wine, and add to the pan.

Cook the mushrooms over a medium heat for about 10 minutes, stirring well, then sprinkle over the flour. Cook for 1 minute, stirring continuously, then add the reserved wine. Bring the mixture slowly to the boil, then lower the heat and cook, uncovered, for about 10 minutes, stirring occasionally. Add the cream and cook for a further 5–10 minutes. Taste and season accordingly.

Once the meat is cooked to your liking, remove it and place it on a carving board, loosely covered with foil. Let it rest for at least 15 minutes before carving and serving with the mushroom sauce.

Steak pie is the traditional main course on New Year's Day (and also on Christmas Day in my home town of Dundee when my parents were growing up there). Here is a reinvention of the classic pie, and includes black olives, red wine and garlic – not exactly the norm for Dundonians brought up in the 1920s and '30s but truly delicious, nonetheless.

Don't forget to start making the stew the day before.

Steak pie with olives

SERVES 4

25g/1 oz butter

about 2 tablespoons olive oil

900g/2 lb stewing beef (chuck or shoulder), cut into large dice

40g/1½ oz plain flour, seasoned

2 onions, peeled and chopped

2 large carrots, peeled and cut into thick chunks

2 sticks of celery, chopped

2 fat garlic cloves, peeled and chopped

350ml/12 fl oz hot beef stock

250ml/9 fl oz red wine

1 heaped tablespoon tomato purée

1 tablespoon Worcestershire sauce

salt and freshly ground black pepper

200g/7 oz black olives

200g/7 oz puff pastry (ready-rolled)

1 small free-range egg, beaten

Preheat the oven to 150°C/300°F/Gas 2.

Heat the butter and 1 tablespoon of the oil in a large casserole. Toss the meat in the well-seasoned flour and then brown all over in the fat, in 2–3 batches (you may need a little extra oil). Remove with a slotted spoon and put to one side.

Add 1 tablespoon oil to the casserole, then add the onions, carrots, celery and garlic. Gently fry for 5 minutes until softened, then return the meat to the pan. Add the hot stock, wine, tomato purée and Worcestershire sauce. Season with salt and pepper, stir and bring to the boil. Cover tightly and cook in the preheated oven for 1¾–2 hours, stirring once. Near the end of the cooking time, add the olives and check and adjust the seasoning.

Tip the contents of the casserole into a 1.7 litre/3 pint pie dish, cool completely then refrigerate overnight. Next day, remove from the fridge 30 minutes before cooking.

Preheat the oven to 220°C/425°F/Gas 7.

Cut a long strip off the rolled-out pastry. Wet your fingers lightly and dampen the edges of the pie dish. Place the pastry strip round the rim of the pie dish, then brush with the beaten egg. Place the remaining pastry over the top of the meat and press down to seal the edges. Trim off any excess pastry and crimp the edges between thumb and forefinger. Brush with beaten egg and snip a hole with scissors in the middle.

Bake in the preheated oven for 30–35 minutes until puffed up and golden brown. You might need to lay a piece of foil lightly over the surface of the pie for the last 10 minutes to prevent burning. Serve piping hot with stir-fried cabbage or green beans.

This is a wonderful and very easy dish that is perfect for a winter's day. I like to serve it with a butter bean mash which I make by mashing potatoes with a drained can of butter beans, enriching it with some hot milk and a good glug of extra virgin olive oil. Roast leeks or stir-fried cabbage is all you need to complete a comforting and truly tasty dish.

Lamb shanks with port and thyme

SERVES 4

4 lamb shanks (weighing about
   1.5kg/3 lb 5 oz altogether)
25g/1 oz plain flour, seasoned
3 tablespoons olive oil
1 onion, peeled and chopped
2 leeks, cleaned and chopped
1 fennel bulb, trimmed and
   chopped
2 sticks of celery, chopped
3 garlic cloves, peeled and
   chopped
100ml/3$\frac{1}{2}$ fl oz port, plus
   1 tablespoon
200ml/7 fl oz hot lamb stock
2–3 thick sprigs of thyme
salt and freshly ground black
   pepper

Preheat the oven to 150°C/300°F/Gas 2.

Place the shanks in a large freezer bag with the seasoned flour and shake well to coat.

Heat 2 tablespoons of the oil in a large casserole and, once hot, add the shanks and brown all over. Set to one side.

Add the remaining oil to the pan and gently fry the vegetables and garlic, adding a little more oil if necessary.

Return the lamb to the casserole and add the 100ml/3$\frac{1}{2}$ fl oz port and the hot stock. Bring to the boil, add the thyme, cover tightly and cook in the preheated oven for 2$\frac{3}{4}$–3 hours.

Using a deep ladle, remove as much of the liquid and the vegetables as possible, and place them in the food processor. Discard the thyme sprigs. Whiz until smooth, then return the liquid to the casserole with the lamb and the remaining 1 tablespoon of port. Taste and season with salt and pepper, then reheat to piping hot and serve.

The crunchy oats and whisky in this glorious pudding are reminiscent of cranachan which is a gorgeous mix of cream, crowdie (a traditional crofters' cottage cheese), oatmeal, berries, whisky and honey. Instead of using traditional crowdie and cream, this recipe uses clotted cream.

Brenda Leddy has been making clotted cream at her farm at Stichill near Kelso in the Borders for some fifteen years. Having gone to Jersey for a holiday with her husband twenty-five years ago, they fell in love with the island's cattle and ended up buying a cow and calf. Now she has a herd of nearly 150 cattle and makes butter, cheese and the most fabulous clotted cream, all of which she sells at farmers' markets in the Borders and Edinburgh. Scottish people have taken a little time to become accustomed to clotted cream as we were not brought up with it, but to which better country to introduce its delights than to the land of scones and cakes!

For Ne'er Day, frozen raspberries or brambles are fine, but it is wonderful in the summer with fresh berries.

Clotted cream cranachan

SERVES 6

2 × 170g tubs clotted cream
75g/2³/₄ oz jumbo oatflakes
75g/2³/₄ oz light muscovado sugar
about 2 tablespoons whisky
500g/1 lb 2 oz mixed berries such
    as brambles (blackberries),
    raspberries, strawberries

Preheat the grill to hot. Tip the cream into a bowl and stir.

Place the oats and sugar on a sheet of foil, then toast under the preheated grill. Watch them constantly, removing and shaking them about, or forking through them every 10–20 seconds or so. After a couple of minutes, the sugar will have caramelised and the oats will be golden. Remember to watch them like a hawk – if they cook for too long, they will burn. Remove and leave to cool.

When cool, loosely break up the mixture between your fingers as you add the crunchy oats to the cream. Add the whisky and stir to combine. Tip the mixture into a serving bowl and chill well.

Serve with berries – and extra whisky, if you like.

This is a wonderful pudding that can be made either with fresh fruit in summer or – for New Year's Day – with thawed frozen fruit. It can also be made with brambles (blackberries) or loganberries instead of tayberries, and blueberries instead of blackcurrants.

When it emerges from the oven, the fruit is bubbling in a puddle of crimson juices and the mascarpone is oozing out seductively from a light cobbler-like scone topping. Because the mascarpone is there, nestled between fruit and scone, you do not need any cream with this. It is a gloriously self-contained pudding.

And before you ask – a slump does just that.

Tayberry and blackcurrant slump

SERVES 6

450g/1 lb tayberries
250g/9 oz blackcurrants
50g/1¾ oz golden caster sugar

FOR THE TOPPING
175g/6 oz self-raising flour, sifted
1 teaspoon baking powder
50g/1¾ oz golden caster sugar
grated zest and juice of
   1 unwaxed lemon
50g/1¾ oz butter, melted
1 large free-range egg, beaten
1 × 250g tub mascarpone

Place the berries and currants in a pan with the sugar and heat very slowly until the sugar is dissolved and the juices run. Tip into an ovenproof dish and allow to cool.

Preheat the oven to 220°C/425°F/Gas 7.

For the topping, combine the flour, baking powder and sugar, then stir in the lemon zest. Add the melted butter, egg and lemon juice and combine gently.

Tip the mascarpone into a bowl and beat until smooth, then drop 6 spoonfuls on to the fruit mixture; resist the urge to join them all together.

Cover each blob with a spoonful of the scone mixture: don't worry if it doesn't cover the mascarpone blob exactly; it will spread out a little as it cooks anyway.

Bake in the preheated oven for about 20 minutes or until the fruit is bubbling and the mascarpone is oozing out from the golden-brown crusted topping. Allow to cool for 5 minutes then serve.

Tablet is as Scottish as mince. And thought of as fondly. Rather like fudge with a bite to it, it is the first thing to sell out at fêtes or church fairs. This version has a gorgeous flavour of white chocolate and cardamom which I think elevates this familiar Scots sweetie to sophisticated dinner party or celebration fare. It is extremely important to follow the method of this to the letter, otherwise it might burn. Stirring constantly might be hard work but the results are worth it, believe me.

White chocolate and cardamom tablet

MAKES about 36 pieces

125g/4½ oz unsalted butter

1kg/2¼ lb golden granulated sugar

300ml/½ pint full-fat milk

a pinch of salt

200ml/7 fl oz condensed milk (this is half a regular can)

100g/3½ oz quality white chocolate, grated

7–8 cardamom pods, snipped open and seeds crushed (about 1 teaspoon)

Butter a 23 × 33cm/9 × 13 in Swiss-roll tin.

Place the butter in a large, heavy-based saucepan (a reliable one) and melt slowly. Add the sugar, milk and salt, and stir until the sugar is dissolved, stirring occasionally. Bring to the boil and simmer over a fairly high heat for 8–10 minutes, stirring often, getting into all the corners.

Add the condensed milk, chocolate and cardamom and simmer for 8–10 minutes over a medium-high heat, stirring constantly. If the phone rings, ignore it.

After 8 minutes, remove the pan from the heat, and test the contents for readiness: it should be at the 'soft ball' stage which means that when you drop a little of the mixture into a cup of very cold water, it will form a soft ball that you can pick up between your fingers. If you are using a sugar thermometer, it should register 115°C/240°F.

Remove the mixture from the heat at once and beat with an electric beater (set at medium speed) for 4–5 minutes (or by hand for 10 minutes) until the mixture begins to stiffen a little and become ever so slightly grainy. Immediately pour it into the prepared tin and leave to cool.

Mark the tablet into tiny squares (it is rich!) when it is almost cold. When it is completely cold, remove it from the tin and store in an airtight container or wrap in waxed paper.

To a haggis

THERE IS NO SUCH THING as a quiet Burns Supper. No matter where it takes place – in a church hall, local hostelry or one's own home – it is not, by nature, sedate. Part of Scottish culture for many years, the ritual was begun by friends of the poet Robert Burns after his death in 1796 as a tribute to his memory. And although the basic format of the evening has remained unchanged over the years (the Selkirk Grace, the Immortal Memory, the Toast to the Lassies, its Response and so on), the food has moved with the times, while adhering more or less to the soup, haggis, pudding formula. And, as for the drink, with obligatory whisky for all the toasts (of which there are many), is it little wonder the evening is far from quiet?

Haggis is the central point of Burns Suppers, not only because it is revered as Scotland's national dish but because of Burns' poem 'To A Haggis'. During the third verse, the kilted reciter ceremoniously stabs the haggis and the euphoric guests gaze admiringly as its 'gushing entrails' are revealed. In the bard's own words: 'And then O what a glorious sight, Warm-reekin, rich.'

At this point in the proceedings, I imagine most vegetarians would be having an attack of the vapours, so, to compensate, there is now that most wonderful oxymoron, the vegetarian haggis – action-packed and stuffed full of nuts, lentils and beans. Personally, I would rather proffer veggie guests a wild mushroom risotto or a cheese soufflé but, if necessary, they too can eat haggis. Haggis needs not be served as a main course these days. I like to serve little tartlets of haggis as canapés, then serve a game or beef dish for the main course. A rich pudding, such as trifle or cloutie dumpling, is, of course, traditional but since in January Seville oranges are at their best, a tangy fresh Seville orange tart or steamed marmalade pudding seems perfect.

Then, once the plates are cleared and the glasses refilled for the toasts, you will very soon begin to appreciate why Burns Suppers are noisy affairs – especially when the accordions begin to limber up for the ceilidh. The suppers are not only fitting tributes to the bard, they are outrageously good fun, highly entertaining – and hopefully delicious. But, above all, never quiet.

During the autumn, you should, of course, use fresh chanterelles instead of dried: thoroughly clean about 250g/9 oz and add them with the onion and garlic at the beginning. Dried porcini will also work well.

Serve this as a vegetarian main course or as a side dish to roast chicken, venison or beef.

Barley risotto with chanterelles

SERVES 6

1 × 40g packet of dried
   chanterelles
850ml/1½ pints hot vegetable
   (or chicken) stock
75g/2¾ oz unsalted butter
2 fat garlic cloves, peeled and
   chopped
1 large onion, peeled and
   chopped
500g/1 lb 2 oz pearl barley
1 tablespoon mushroom ketchup,
   optional
1 teaspoon salt and plenty of
   freshly ground black pepper
2 tablespoons freshly chopped
   flat parsley
coarsely grated Parmesan,
   optional

Rinse the dried mushrooms, then soak them in the hot stock for about 30 minutes.

Preheat the oven to 170°C/325°F/Gas 3.

Melt the butter in a large flameproof casserole, then gently fry the garlic and onion for about 10 minutes or until softened.

Add the barley, stir well to coat with the butter, then add the mushroom ketchup, if using, soaked mushrooms and stock. Bring to the boil, stirring, then season with the salt and pepper.

Cover tightly, remove from the heat and place in the preheated oven for about 30–35 minutes or until the liquid is all absorbed.

Remove, taste for seasoning and stir in the parsley. Serve hot, with or without grated Parmesan.

Instead of making your own tartlet cases, you can cheat and buy good-quality, ready-made ones; even top chefs do this so don't feel you are allowing culinary standards to slip. It will give you more time to spend on the rest of the evening's fare. But home-made are, of course, best.

The quality of haggis you buy is important; see page 160.

Haggis tartlets with red onion marmalade

MAKES 36 canapé-size tartlets

1 haggis

FOR THE PASTRY
175g/6 oz plain flour, sifted
25g/1 oz freshly grated Parmesan
½ teaspoon salt
115g/4 oz unsalted butter, cubed
1 medium free-range egg
about ½ tablespoon olive oil

FOR THE RED ONION MARMALADE
3 medium red onions, peeled and
    finely chopped
2 tablespoons olive oil
2 tablespoons red wine or cider
    vinegar
4 tablespoons red wine or cider
1 tablespoon dark muscovado
    sugar
salt and freshly ground black
    pepper

For the pastry, combine the flour, cheese, salt and butter and whiz until blended. Then add the egg through the feeder tube and a little oil – enough to let you bring it together in your hands. Wrap in clingfilm, and chill in the refrigerator for an hour.

Roll out the dough and fill 36 tartlet cases. Chill well for at least 30 minutes.

Preheat the oven to190°C/375°F/Gas 5.

Prick the bases of the tartlets, then bake in the preheated oven for 12–15 minutes or until cooked. Reheat to warm before the haggis is added.

For the marmalade, sauté the onions in the oil for 15–20 minutes until softened. Add the vinegar, wine or cider and sugar and increase the heat. Once bubbling, lower the heat to a simmer, cover and cook gently for 10 minutes. Then cook, uncovered, for about 20 minutes or until thick. Season to taste with salt and pepper, then allow to cool.

To assemble, heat the haggis: I wrap it in foil and place it in an oven preheated to 180°C/350°F/Gas 4 for about 45 minutes or until it is piping hot. Slit open the haggis and spoon some into each warm pastry case. Top with a dollop of marmalade and serve at once.

You can use either regular smoked haddock fillets (or, indeed, finnan haddock) or Arbroath smokies, but for the latter do not cook in the milk since they have been hot-smoked and are therefore already cooked. Just warm the milk.

This is a variation on Provence's wonderful dish of salt cod and potato pounded with garlic, olive oil and warm milk to make a gorgeous purée which is eaten with black olives and pain de campagne. As a starter at your Burns Supper, serve this with olives and good chewy sourdough bread, fresh or toasted.

Smoked haddock brandade

SERVES 6

about 200g/7 oz potatoes
salt and feshly ground black
   pepper
500g/1 lb 2 oz undyed smoked
   haddock fillets (or 1 pair
   Arbroath smokies
    about 600g/1 lb 5 oz)
200ml/7 fl oz milk
2 bay leaves
2 garlic cloves, peeled and
   crushed
2 tablespoons fresh flat parsley or
   lovage leaves
juice of 1 lemon
about 5 tablespoons extra virgin
   olive oil

Peel and cook the potatoes in boiling, salted water until tender, then drain thoroughly.

At the same time, place the fish in a pan with the milk and bay leaves. Bring slowly to the boil. For smoked haddock, simmer for about 3 minutes then remove and cover. Leave to stand for 10–15 minutes. If you are using smokies, remove the pan from the heat the minute you see bubbles, cover and leave for 10-15 minutes.

Drain the fish, reserving the milk, then flake it, ensuring there are no bones or skin. Discard the bay leaves. Place the fish in the food processor together with the potato, garlic, parsley or lovage, the lemon juice and the reserved warm milk. Process briefly; then, with the machine running, add enough oil to give a soft, creamy consistency (like mashed potatoes).

Check the seasoning, then turn the brandade into a bowl and cool to room temperature before serving with olives and bread.

The easiest way to remove the flesh from Arbroath smokies (which, since they are hot-smoked, can be eaten as they are, without further cooking) is to warm them slightly first: either do this in a microwave for a couple of minutes, or in a low oven, loosely wrapped in foil, for about 10 minutes. Then lay the fish on a board, skin-side down, and press your thumb along the length of the bone. This long bone should come away easily in your hand and then the flesh can be flaked.

Use olives stored in oil not brine; Kalamata are the best.

Arbroath smokies and parsnip salad

SERVES 4

about 700g/1 lb 9 oz parsnips, peeled
1 pair Arbroath smokies
mixed salad leaves
3 tablespoons black olives

FOR THE DRESSING
4 tablespoons olive oil
juice of 1 lemon
2 tablespoons finely chopped chives
salt and freshly ground black pepper

Cut the parsnips into matchsticks, drop into boiling water for just a couple of minutes until they are just tender (neither hard nor too soft). Drain and set on one side.

Remove the flesh from the smokies and flake.

Arrange the salad leaves in a large bowl and scatter over the olives.

Whisk or shake the dressing ingredients together and season with salt and pepper to taste, then pour over the parsnips while they are still warm, stirring to coat them.

Tip the dressed parsnips over the salad leaves and top with the flaked smokies. Serve at once with plenty of warm bread.

You can cook the rumbledethumps earlier in the day and reheat it in the oven for about 20 minutes to warm through.

As for the haggis, avoid any supermarket own-label, unless it is made by a well-known name such as Macsweens. All the supermarket ones I have tried are either too livery (which is not actually authentic) or just plain dull. Get one from a reliable butcher – preferably one who still makes them in natural casing instead of plastic. Rumledethumps – my mum's speciality – is good served with all sorts of meat dishes from steak pie or roasts to plain old mince. It is also perfect for vegetarians who could eat it with a veggie haggis or on its own.

Rumbledethumps with haggis

SERVES 4

1 large haggis

FOR THE RUMBLEDETHUMPS
600g/1 lb 5 oz large potatoes
400g/14 oz turnip (swede)
salt and freshly ground black
**   pepper**
250g/9 oz cabbage (preferably
**   Savoy), shredded**
75g/ 2³/₄ oz unsalted butter
25g/1 oz Cheddar cheese, grated

Preheat the oven to 180°C/350°F/Gas 4.

To cook the haggis, wrap it tightly in foil, place it in an ovenproof dish (one that gives a snug fit) and cook in the preheated oven for about 45 minutes per 450g/1 lb – or until piping hot.

Meanwhile, peel and chop the potatoes and turnip, and cook in boiling, salted water until tender, then drain thoroughly. Return the vegetables to the pan.

Gently cook the cabbage with 50g/1³/₄ oz butter until tender, but still vivid green. (I melt the butter in a microwave bowl, toss in the cabbage, cover and cook for about 3 minutes.)

Tip the cabbage and butter into the vegetable saucepan and mash everything together with the remaining 25g/1 oz butter. Season generously with salt and pepper to taste.

Place the vegetables in an ovenproof dish and top with the cheese. Cover and place in the preheated oven for about 25 minutes. Then remove the cover and continue to cook for a further 15–20 minutes until bubbling and hot.

To serve, slit the haggis down the middle and spoon the gushing entrails on to warmed plates. Serve with the rumbledethumps.

*This is good served with any game, poultry or red meat dish,
and I particularly like it with venison, pork or chicken. It can be
prepared in the morning and simply covered with foil and
reheated in a medium oven (180°C/350°F/Gas 4) for about
30 minutes or until piping hot.*

Potato and juniper gratin

SERVES 6

**500g/1 lb 2 oz large potatoes,
  peeled**
500g/1 lb 2 oz parsnips, peeled
300ml/10 fl oz double cream
100ml/3½ fl oz milk
**2 teaspoons salt and some freshly
  ground black pepper**
20–24 juniper berries
butter

Preheat the oven to 180°C/350°F/Gas 4.

Slice the vegetables very thinly indeed (I use the slicing blade on my food processor), then place them in a heavy pan with the cream, milk and salt. Crush the juniper berries and sprinkle in, then season with pepper.

Bring slowly to the boil, then simmer gently for 2 minutes, stirring carefully to prevent sticking – but not vigorously enough to break up the vegetables. Tip into a buttered shallow gratin dish, dot with butter and bake in the preheated oven for about 1 hour or until the vegetables are tender and the top tinged with golden brown. Serve very warm.

This extraordinarily simple dish is very tasty. It also sums up the current food ethos: few ingredients (but top quality) and cooked simply to bring out the full flavours. This should be easy in Scotland where we have such fine produce; there is no excuse at all for an insidious dependence on processed food at all. This sublime venison dish takes little over half an hour from start to finish!

Serve with a rich, creamy potato gratin (see page 161) and a lightly dressed green salad – preferably made with watercress, young spinach and rocket.

Venison with oat and herb crust

SERVES 6

25g/1 oz butter

3 tablespoons olive oil

1 kg/2¼ lb boneless venison (e.g. sirloin roast), trimmed

salt and freshly ground black pepper

100g/3½ oz medium (or half medium, half pinhead) oatmeal

3 tablespoons finely chopped parsley and thyme

Preheat the oven to 230°C/450°F/Gas 8.

Heat the butter and 1 tablespoon of the oil in a roasting tin on the hob until hot. Season the venison with salt and pepper, and brown all over (which will take 4–5 minutes). Remove the meat and let it cool for 5–10 minutes.

Mix together the oatmeal, herbs, oil and plenty of salt and pepper, then press this all over the meat. Return it to the roasting tin and roast in the preheated oven for 15–20 minutes (approximately 8 minutes per 500g/1 lb 2 oz), then leave in a warm place or a low oven (150°C/300°F/Gas 2) to rest for at least 10 minutes before carving.

This recipe is from Fiona Bird, a talented cook who lives in Kirriemuir, not far from Glamis where the Pattullos farm their sea kale between January and March, before the asparagus season begins (see page 46).

Fiona serves the beef with a tattie and broccoli mash.

Poached beef fillet with buttered sea kale

SERVES 2

1 litre/1¾ pints beef stock

225g/8 oz fillet of beef, trimmed
   and tied

25g/1 oz butter

1 shallot, peeled and chopped

1 garlic clove, peeled and crushed

½ small stick of celery, diced

1 large red pepper, seeded and
   sliced

salt and freshly ground black
   pepper

FOR THE SEA KALE

1 shallot, peeled and chopped

3 tablespoons white wine vinegar

225g/8 oz chilled unsalted butter,
   diced

salt and freshly ground black
   pepper

a squeeze of lemon juice

115g/4 oz sea kale
   (about 6 pieces)

Preheat the oven to 190°C/375°F/Gas 5.

Pour all but 150ml/5 fl oz stock into a deep casserole dish. Heat to almost boiling. Lower the beef into it and cover with foil. Cook in the preheated oven for 20–25 minutes.

Meanwhile, melt the butter and sauté the shallot, garlic and celery for 5 minutes, then add the red pepper and remaining stock. Simmer for 10 minutes, then whiz in a food processor until nearly smooth. Check the seasoning, decant into a bowl and keep warm.

For the sea kale, place the shallot in a pan with the vinegar and 3 tablespoons water. Bring to the boil and reduce until there is about 2 tablespoons liquid. Lower the heat and gradually whisk in the butter, one piece at a time, until you have a smooth, thick and glossy sauce. Season with salt and pepper and add a squeeze of lemon juice.

Meanwhile, steam the sea kale (or cook in an asparagus kettle) for 3–4 minutes. Drain and place on a warm serving dish and spoon a little of the butter sauce over.

To serve the beef, slice the fillet in half and serve with a puddle of the red pepper sauce and some mash.

This is a truly delicious casserole – a great family favourite –
that relies not only on best lamb but, of course, on quality black
pudding made by your own local butcher.

Lamb casserole
with a black pudding crust

Serves 4

2 tablespoons olive oil

25g/1 oz butter

750g/1 lb 10 oz lamb shoulder,
 diced

1 heaped tablespoon flour,
 seasoned

1 onion, peeled and chopped

1 medium leek, finely sliced

2 garlic cloves, peeled and
 chopped

2 fat sprigs of rosemary

150ml/5 fl oz gutsy red wine

150ml/5 fl oz lamb stock

200g/7 oz skinned black pudding,
 thinly sliced

Preheat the oven to 170°C/325°F/Gas 3.

Heat 1 tablespoon of the oil with the butter in a large casserole until hot. Toss the lamb in a large bag of seasoned flour then add to the fat, in two batches, until brown all over. Remove the meat with a slotted spoon and put to one side.

Add the remaining oil and gently fry the onion, leek and garlic until softened. Return the meat to the casserole with the rosemary, wine and stock and bring to the boil. Cover and cook in the preheated oven for 1–1½ hours, stirring once.

Remove from the oven, discard the rosemary and check the seasoning. (At this stage, you can chill the lamb to remove any surface fat before adding the black pudding crust. If you do this, take the casserole out of the fridge early to return to room temperature before placing in the oven again.)

Increase the oven temperature to 190°C/375°F/Gas 5. Place the black pudding on top of the meat, overlapping the slices slightly. Brush with a little olive oil and replace in the oven for about 25 minutes until the stew is bubbling and the top crusty. Serve with either mashed potatoes or pappardelle and a green vegetable.

This is a lovely citrus tart, so called because Dundee is famous for its marmalade. Being so far away from Spain where Seville oranges grow, it seems strange that my home town is famous for what I believe is the best marmalade in the world. Put it down to Scottish thrift: the Keiller family of Dundee received a consignment of bitter instead of sweet oranges, and rather than throw them away, they turned them into marmalade.

Seville oranges are only available in January and February, which is fine for Burns Suppers, but because I like to eat this wonderful tart at other times of the year, I also make it with pink grapefruit. Adding the grated zest of one grapefruit for extra flavour.

Dundee tart

SERVES 8

200ml/7 fl oz Seville orange juice
   (about 4 Seville oranges), or
   pink grapefruit juice
200g/7 oz golden caster sugar
5 large free-range eggs, beaten
200ml/7 fl oz double cream

FOR THE PASTRY

150g/5½ oz plain flour, sifted
25g/1 oz golden caster sugar
75g/2¾ oz ground almonds
115g/4 oz chilled butter, diced
1 large free-range egg

To make the pastry place the flour, sugar, ground almonds and butter in a food processor and whiz briefly, then add the egg through the feeder tube while the machine is running. Bring the dough together with your hands, wrap in clingfilm and chill. Roll out to fit a buttered deep 24cm/9½in tart tin. Prick the base and chill well – preferably overnight.

Preheat the oven to 200°C/400°F/Gas 6. Fill the tart tin with foil and baking beans and bake in the preheated oven for 15 minutes. Remove the foil and beans, continue to bake for 5 minutes and then remove and cool. Reduce the oven temperature to 170°C/325°F/Gas 3.

For the filling, strain the juice into a bowl and beat in the sugar until dissolved. Push the eggs through a sieve placed over the bowl containing the orange juice, add the cream and combine. Pour the mixture into a jug.

To fill the tart, I find the easiest way is to place the tart case on a baking sheet in the oven and pull out the oven rack. Very slowly pour in the mixture and then carefully push the oven rack back in. Bake for about 40–45 minutes or until the filling is just firm: if you shake the tin, it should still wobble a little in the middle.

Allow the tart to cool, then remove it to a serving plate.

The end of January is the perfect time for this lovely homely pudding, using the first of the early (forced) rhubarb which is not only less coarse than the later rhubarb but often a prettier colour – more pink than greenish.

Similar to a crumble, a crisp is a North American dish which often uses rolled oats to add to the crunch. Serve this with thick cream or custard. Or both.

Rhubarb and oat crisp

SERVES 6

900g/2 lb rhubarb (trimmed weight), chopped

75g/2¾ oz golden granulated sugar

100g/3½ oz plain flour, sifted

75g/2¾ oz porridge oats

125g/4½ oz light muscovado sugar

125g/4½ oz butter, diced

1 teaspoon ground cinnamon

Preheat the oven to 190°C/375°F/Gas 5.

Place the rhubarb in an ovenproof dish and sprinkle over the sugar. Shake the dish a little, to distribute the sugar throughout.

Place the flour, oats and sugar in a bowl, then rub in the butter until the mixture resembles breadcrumbs. Stir in the cinnamon.

Tip this over the rhubarb and pack down lightly.

Bake in the preheated oven for 40–45 minutes or until the rhubarb is tender; you may need to place a piece of foil lightly on top after 35 minutes or so to prevent the topping browning too much.

Cool for at least 15 minutes, then serve warm.

Use thick shortbread fingers for this, not thin petticoat tail

rounds. You can also use the chocolate shortbread on page 133.

Shortbread ice cream with sticky bananas

SERVES 4

1 × 500ml tub of quality vanilla
   ice cream
115g/4 oz shortbread fingers,
   roughly chopped into large
   chunks
4 bananas, peeled, cut into 4
   lengthways
lemon juice
75g/2¾ oz dark muscovado sugar
75g/2¾ oz unsalted butter
150ml/5 fl oz double cream

Preheat the oven to 220°C/425°F/Gas 7.

Soften the ice cream very slightly, then stir in the shortbread – not too vigorously as you want chunks, not crumbs.

Spoon into a freezer dish, cover and refreeze.

Place the bananas in a shallow dish and sprinkle with a little lemon juice. Place the sugar, butter and cream in a saucepan and bring slowly to the boil. Bubble away for about 3 minutes, then pour all over the bananas.

Place the dish in the preheated oven for 10–15 minutes, until sticky and piping hot.

Eat with scoops of the ice cream.

Chitterin' food

CHITTERIN' FOOD – or comfort food – comes in many shapes and sizes but in Scotland it is invariably in the shape of a soup pot, casserole dish or pudding basin. As for size, just think Desperate Dan and his Cow Pie rather than Gwendolen's dainty bread and butter in *The Importance of Being Earnest*. Cold weather gives you a real appetite.

As children, we were always given a 'shivery bite' after emerging, shaking with cold and dripping wet, from the icy waters into the even icier air, whether the swimming took place at a public pool or – more probably – in the sea. Also known in Scotland as a 'chattering bite' or 'chitterin' piece', this was to stave off the chattering of your teeth or the shivering of your entire body. Rather appropriate, really. Although shivery bites were small snacks such as biscuits, rolls or sandwiches, comfort food can encompass all sorts of dishes from a simple soup or stew to a satisfyingly rich steamed pudding or teeth-defyingly chewy treacle tart. This is food that will stoke up your inner warmth; but it is also food for the soul.

There is nothing minimalist about comfort food and there is no place here for food arranged on the plate. One large dish is placed in the middle of the table and everyone tucks in with gusto. A mound of garlicky *Langoustine mash* or rich, creamy *Crab risotto* fit the bill perfectly – top Scottish ingredients converted into delicious, nourishing and tempting food. *Selkirk bannock bread-and-butter pudding* is one of the nicest variants of that favourite nursery pud I know. And the *7-cup pudding* is a saunter down memory lane, for this is one of the many puddings I used to adore as a child; it comes a close second to my Auntie Mue's glorious Cloutie Dumpling in the 'Memorable Puddings of My Life'.

Chitterin' food can be eaten at any time of the day – or night. But even in the unusual circumstances of a warm Scottish summer, I highly recommend a brisk walk outside first, to stimulate the appetite. For there is no use tackling comfort food when feeling only vaguely hungry. You want to be utterly ravenous: perhaps not so hungry that you could wolf down a Cow Pie, horns and all, but certainly a good portion of *Clapshot shepherd's pie*.

That's Bonnet as in cheese, not as in the tam-o'-shanter worn by some be-kilted Scots on their heads. Bonnet is a lovely, firm goat's cheese made in Ayrshire; another hard but medium-strength goat's cheese would substitute well.

Roast pumpkin and Bonnet lasagne

SERVES 4

1 small pumpkin or 1 medium butternut squash (about 1kg/2¼ lb), peeled and cubed

3 tablespoons olive oil

225g/8 oz spinach, washed

8 tablespoons passata (thin tomato purée)

6 sheets of dried (pre-cooked) lasagne

salt and freshly ground black pepper

3–4 thick sprigs of fresh thyme

4 plum tomatoes, thinly sliced

150g/5½ oz Bonnet goat's cheese, grated

Preheat the oven to 200°C/400°F/Gas 6.

Tip the pumpkin or squash into a roasting tin and turn it in 2 tablespoons of the oil. Roast in the preheated oven for about 30 minutes or until tender. Cool. Reduce the oven temperature to 180°C/350°F/Gas 4 for the next stage.

Cook the spinach briefly in a very little water, drain thoroughly, chop roughly and pat with kitchen paper until thoroughly dry.

Place 4 tablespoons of the passata in a small, oiled lasagne dish, then top with half the lasagne. Tip in the pumpkin or squash, then season with salt and pepper and sprinkle over the thyme leaves. Top with another layer of lasagne, then the remaining passata; finally add the sliced tomatoes and the spinach. Season well with salt and pepper. Sprinkle over the cheese, and pat down gently. Drizzle over the remaining oil.

Cover with oiled foil and bake in the preheated oven for about 30 minutes, then remove the foil and continue to bake for about 15 minutes, or until the lasagne is bubbling and golden.

Serve warm with salad and bread.

Broad beans have a wonderful affinity with blue cheese.
I adore this simple risotto enriched with Humphrey Errington's
fabulous cow's milk blue cheese, Dunsyre Blue. If you cannot get
Dunsyre Blue, another farmhouse cow's milk blue cheese will do.

It is so much better if tender young broad beans are used;
older ones can be used only if you blanch them first and then
slip off their tough skins. For the amount of podded beans
required in the recipe, you will need about 1kg/2¼ lb beans in
the pod. In the winter, frozen broad beans are ideal since they
are perfectly tender and have no tough outer casing.

Broad bean and Dunsyre Blue risotto

SERVES 3–4

50g/1¾ oz butter

1 tablespoon olive oil

1 onion, peeled and finely chopped

2 garlic cloves, peeled and finely chopped

1 small fennel bulb (or ½ a large one), trimmed, finely chopped

250g/9 oz risotto rice (arborio, carnaroli or vialone nano)

1 glass dry white wine

about 700ml/1¼ pints hot chicken or vegetable stock

350g/12 oz young broad beans

salt and freshly ground black pepper

60g/2¼ oz Dunsyre Blue cheese, chopped or crumbled

2 tablespoons chopped herbs (any combination of mint, dill, marjoram, summer savory)

Heat the butter and oil in a large saucepan, then gently fry the onion, garlic and fennel for about 10 minutes, stirring, until golden. Add the rice and stir well to coat, about 1 minute.

Add the wine and stir over a high heat until it is completely absorbed. Now, over a medium heat, start adding the hot stock, ladle by ladle, only adding the next when all the liquid has been absorbed. Stir well.

After the first 5 minutes or so, add the broad beans and continue to cook over a medium heat, until the rice is tender yet with some bite to it (up to 20 minutes); by this stage it will all be nicely creamy. Season with pepper but not yet with salt. Now add the cheese and most of the fresh herbs. Stir well, cover tightly and leave for 5–10 minutes, then stir again. Check and adjust seasoning; adding salt now, depending on how salty the cheese is.

Sprinkle over the remaining herbs and serve in warm bowls.

If you have a good relationship with your fishmonger, ask him to cook a fresh crab for you; you can then tackle the task of extracting the meat at home. Better still, ask him to do everything – removing all the meat and separating out the white meat from the brown. If, however, you are unsure whether your fishmonger dresses his own crab, then buy a live one and boil it yourself. (For this dish, you will probably need 2 large crabs.) What is called 'dressed crab' is sometimes bulked out with alien adjuncts such as breadcrumbs or even digestive biscuits – which although indispensable when dunking at teatime, have no place in this comforting risotto. For the wine, I like a Pinot grigio which is good in the dish – and your glass.

Crab risotto

SERVES 4

about 750ml/25 fl oz fish (or light chicken) stock

a large pinch of saffron threads

25g/1 oz butter

2 tablespoons olive oil

1 medium onion, peeled and finely chopped

1 large stick of celery, finely chopped

300g /10$^{1}/_{2}$ oz risotto rice (arborio, carnaroli, vialone nano)

250ml/9 fl oz dry white wine

350g/12 oz cooked crab meat

salt and freshly ground black pepper

2 tablespoons freshly chopped parsley or chervil

Heat the stock and add the saffron to soak. I like to keep the pan of stock gently simmering beside the risotto pan.

Heat the butter and oil in the risotto pan, then add the onion and celery and cook gently for about 10 minutes until softened. Add the rice and cook for a minute or so, stirring to coat.

Add the wine, increase the heat, then bubble for a couple of minutes. Now reduce the heat to medium again and gradually add the hot stock, ladle by ladle, stirring well and only adding more liquid once the previous ladleful has been absorbed.

About 15 minutes after the first ladleful of stock is added, add the crab meat and some salt and pepper. Once it is ready – and all or most of the stock has been added (up to 20 minutes) – taste and check the seasoning. Cover tightly, remove from the heat and leave to stand for 5 minutes.

Sprinkle with the parsley or chervil and serve straight from the pan with a tossed green salad: I like a mixture of young sorrel and watercress.

This is pure hedonistic heaven. A mound of buttery mashed potatoes with some lightly sautéed langoustines added…well, it beats hot water bottles and bed socks for me.

Because they are expensive, I have allowed three langoustines each, but if you can afford more, sling them in!

Langoustine mash

SERVES 4

1 kg/2¼ lb floury potatoes (see
    page 18), peeled and chopped
salt and freshly ground black
    pepper
100g/3½ oz butter
100ml/3½ fl oz milk, heated
12 live langoustines
2 tablespoons olive oil
2 garlic cloves, peeled and
    crushed, optional
1 tablespoon freshly chopped
    flat parsley, optional

Boil the potatoes in salted water until tender, then drain really well. Mash them with the butter and hot milk. Season with salt and pepper to taste.

Meanwhile, blanch the langoustines (to kill them) by plunging them into a large pan of boiling, salted water. Bring them back to the boil, then immediately tip them into a colander and place under the cold running tap to arrest cooking.

Once they are cool enough to handle, remove the shells and de-vein them (slit the backs with the tip of a knife and remove the intestinal tract). You should now have 12 plump langoustine tails.

Heat the oil in a frying pan until hot, add the langoustines and garlic, if using, and cook for about 1½–2 minutes, turning once. Remove and tip into the mash and gently stir through.

Serve in warm bowls, sprinkled with freshly chopped parsley, if desired.

Based on Tuscany's sugo de lepre – hare sauce served with pappardelle (wide flat pasta ribbons) – my recipe is for rabbit which is far cheaper and, unlike hare, available all year. Rabbit stew used to be an everyday dish all over Scotland.

This can be made the day before, then simply reheated to serve with the pasta, together with a salad of floppy lettuce in a mustardy vinaigrette.

Pappardelle with rabbit sauce

SERVES 4

4 tablespoons olive oil

1 onion, peeled and chopped

2 garlic cloves, peeled and chopped

2 sticks of celery, chopped

50g/1¾ oz smoked bacon, chopped

6–8 plump rabbit joints

1 tablespoon plain flour

350ml/12 fl oz gutsy red wine

2 sprigs each of thyme and rosemary

salt and freshly ground black pepper

350g/12 oz pappardelle

Heat 2 tablespoons of the oil in a heavy casserole and gently fry the onion, garlic, celery and bacon for 10 minutes, then remove to a dish.

Add another 1 tablespoon of the oil to the pan. Dust the rabbit in the flour and add to the pan. Brown all over, then return the vegetables to the pan with the wine, herb sprigs and some salt and pepper. Bring to the boil, then reduce to a gentle simmer. Cover and cook over a low heat for about 1 hour, stirring once.

When cool, remove the meat from the bones, divide into chunks and return to the pan. Reheat gently until it is piping hot; check seasoning.

Cook the pasta according to the instructions on the packet. Drain and toss in the remaining oil and pile into a warm serving dish. Tip the rabbit sauce over the pasta and serve at once.

This is a hearty lasagne with some good strong flavourings: the lamb meatballs contain mint, cumin and Parmesan, and the cream sauce is spiked with pesto. There is also a gooey surprise in the centre of the lasagne, from the mozzarella. The lasagne can be made in advance, then brought to room temperature and baked just before serving.

Lamb meatball lasagne

SERVES 6–8

2–3 tablespoons olive oil

150ml/5 fl oz double cream

1 × 500g carton of ricotta

100g/3¹/₂ oz freshly grated Parmesan

1 heaped tablespoon pesto sauce

salt and freshly ground black pepper

700g/1 lb 9 oz jar of sugocasa (thick chopped tomatoes)

about 9 sheets dried (pre-cooked) lasagne

150g/5¹/₂ oz mozzarella cheese, thinly sliced

FOR THE MEATBALLS

750g/1 lb 10 oz minced lamb

3 garlic cloves, peeled and chopped

2 heaped tablespoons finely chopped fresh mint

75g/2³/₄ oz freshly grated Parmesan

¹/₄ teaspoon ground cumin

1 large free-range egg

For the meatballs, combine all the ingredients. Form into 20 balls and chill for 30 minutes or so. Then fry in 1–2 tablespoons of the oil until brown all over and just cooked through. Drain on kitchen paper.

Preheat the oven to 200°C/400°F/Gas 6.

Beat together the cream, ricotta, 75g/2³/₄ oz of the Parmesan and the pesto; season well with salt and pepper.

Spread about a quarter of the sugocasa over the base of a large lasagne dish, then top with 3 sheets of lasagne. Put in one-third of the creamy cheese mixture, then half the meatballs. Lay over the mozzarella slices and season with salt and pepper.

Now top with another quarter of the sugocasa, 3 more lasagne sheets, another third of the creamy cheese, then the remaining meatballs. Season well with salt and pepper, and add another quarter of the sugocasa. Finally, place the last 3 sheets of lasagne on top, pour over the rest of the sugocasa, and smooth over the remaining creamy cheese. It will look a complete mess by now, but don't worry as it will sort itself out as it bakes.

Scatter over the remaining Parmesan, and drizzle over the remaining oil. Cover with oiled foil, and bake in the preheated oven for 45 minutes, then remove the foil and continue to cook for about 10–15 minutes until bubbling. Rest for 10 minutes or so before cutting and serving with salad.

Clapshot is an Orcadian potato dish that is not dissimilar to Irish champ or colcannon. It is lovely served as it is, with a cold glass of buttermilk and some thick oatcakes but, as a topping on a shepherd's pie, it is pretty unbeatable. Comfort food at its best.

Clapshot shepherd's pie

SERVES 4

1 tablespoon olive oil

1 medium onion, peeled and
    finely chopped

450g/1 lb beef mince

2 teaspoons plain flour

150ml/5 fl oz hot beef stock

1 tablespoon tomato purée

1 tablespoon Worcestershire
    sauce

1 tablespoon finely chopped
    parsley

salt and freshly ground black
    pepper

400g/14 oz potatoes, peeled and
    chopped

400g/14 oz turnip (swede),
    peeled and chopped

40g/1½ oz butter

1 tablespoon finely chopped
    chives

Heat the oil in a pan, cook the onion gently for about 10 minutes, then increase the heat and add the mince. Brown all over, stirring to break it up. Sprinkle with the flour and add the hot stock. Bring the mixture to the boil, and add the tomato purée, Worcestershire sauce and parsley, and season with salt and pepper. Stir, cover and cook for about 15 minutes, then tip into an ovenproof dish.

Preheat the oven to 180°C/350°F/Gas 4.

For the topping, boil the potatoes and turnip until tender, then drain well. Mash the vegetables with the butter, then add the chives and season with salt and pepper to taste.

Spoon the clapshot over the mince, fork up the top and bake in the preheated oven for 35–40 minutes or until piping hot.

Serve with peas.

This divine and deeply comforting pudding is seriously rich so, tempting though it is to sit with the entire bowl and scoff the lot, try to stick to one portion – with a hefty follow-up of seconds of course. But then desist! At this stage you might feel ready to share it with guests.

For the brownies either use the raspberry chocolate brownies on page 34, or use plain chocolate brownies by following the same recipe but omitting the raspberries and baking for only 35 minutes.

The addition of the orange flower water is by no means essential but does add a wonderfully exotic, elusive flavour.

Raspberry chocolate brownie trifle

SERVES 6

6–8 brownies (the number
   depends on the shape of
   the trifle bowl)
500g/1 lb 2 oz raspberries,
   plus extra to garnish
4–5 tablespoons Drambuie
500g/1 lb 2 oz mascarpone
100g/3½ oz golden caster sugar
3 large free-range eggs, separated
3–4 drops orange flower water,
   optional
50g/1¾ oz plain chocolate,
   coarsely grated

Break each brownie in half and place in the base of a glass trifle bowl. Top with the raspberries and slowly drizzle over the Drambuie.

Beat the mascarpone with the sugar and egg yolks until smooth. Whisk the egg whites until stiff and gently fold into the mascarpone, starting with a small amount to lighten the mixture. Finally, fold in the orange flower water, if using, to taste.

Spread the mascarpone mixture over the brownies and raspberries, cover with foil and refrigerate for about 8 hours or overnight.

To serve, top with the grated chocolate and garnish with extra raspberries.

Much as I love bread-and-butter pudding made from brioche, pain au chocolat or panettone, I find the very best of all is made from Selkirk bannock, that glorious fruited bread made in the Borders. Like panettone, it keeps well and so this is the sort of pudding you can rustle up from a bannock languishing in your larder when you feel in need of comforting fare. Because it already has the dried fruit in it, there is nothing much else you need add – apart from a splash of whisky, which never goes amiss.

Selkirk bannock bread-and-butter pudding with whisky

SERVES 6

about 650g/1 lb 7 oz Selkirk
   bannock, thickly sliced
about 50g/1¾ oz butter, softened
2 large free-range eggs
250ml/9 fl oz milk
150ml/5 fl oz double cream
50g/1¾ oz golden caster sugar
malt whisky, optional

Butter the slices of bannock and lay them in an ovenproof dish.

Whisk together the eggs, milk, cream and sugar, then strain over the bannock. Leave for at least 30 minutes to soak.

Preheat the oven to 180°C/350°F/Gas 4.

Place the dish in a roasting tin which should be half-filled with boiling water and bake in the preheated oven for about 45 minutes or until set but still soft.

Serve warm with a splash of whisky over each portion, if using.

This might not be treacle tart as you know it, but it is treacle tart as I know it, for in Scotland, treacle is just that – black treacle, thick, dark and intense. Golden syrup is also widely used but we call it exactly that. As a child, I had syrup sponge and treacle sponge, syrup tart and treacle tart. Provided you love the rich molasses flavour of treacle, you will – like me – love this tart.

Serve it cold if it is eaten on the day it is made; or barely warmed if it is eaten the next day. A puddle of single cream would not go amiss.

Treacle tart

SERVES 6–8

4 heaped tablespoons golden
    syrup
2 heaped tablespoons black
    treacle
juice and zest of 2 large unwaxed
    lemons
zest of 1 unwaxed lime
40g/1½ oz fresh white
    breadcrumbs
25g/1 oz desiccated coconut

FOR THE PASTRY
100g/3½ oz plain flour, sifted
25g/1 oz golden caster sugar
50g/1¾ oz ground almonds
75g/2¾ oz chilled unsalted
    butter, diced
1 medium free-range egg

For the pastry, place the flour, sugar, ground almonds and butter in a food processor and process briefly. Gradually add the egg through the feeder tube, then gather the dough into a ball, wrap it in clingfilm and chill.

Roll out the dough to fit a 20cm/8 in tart tin with a removable base, prick the base and chill well, preferably overnight.

Preheat the oven to 200°C/400°F/Gas 6.

Blind bake the tart by lining it with foil and beans and baking it in the preheated oven for 15 minutes. Remove the foil and beans, and continue to bake for a further 5 minutes. Remove and cool slightly. Reduce the oven temperature to 170°C/325°F/Gas 3.

Mix together the golden syrup, black treacle, lemon juice and zest and lime zest, breadcrumbs and coconut. Tip the mixture into the tart case and bake for about 30 minutes or until just set.

Let the tart cool before decanting it from the tin.

This is a truly delicious – and incredibly easy – steamed pudding
that, for me, sums up the words comfort food for various reasons.
The taste is divinely sweet and fruity, and the texture is squidgy
and moist and the very sight of it, topped with a glossy crown of
butterscotch sauce, is enough to make me drool.

And it brings back comforting memories, for me, since I used
to adore it as a child. My addition is the butterscotch sauce.

I have found recipes for 7-cup pudding in three old cookery
books – one from 1913, one from 1939 and the last from 1967.
The 1913 one suggests serving it with jam or custard and has no
spices; the 1939 recipe has cinnamon, ginger and a cup of
chopped apple; the latest one is almost the same as mine, but
uses cinnamon and currants instead of mixed spice and sultanas.

7- cup pudding with butterscotch sauce

SERVES 6

1 mug raisins

1 mug sultanas

1 mug self-raising flour

1 mug suet

1 mug fresh breadcrumbs

1 mug light muscovado sugar

1 teaspoon ground cinnamon

1 teaspoon ground mixed spice

1 mug milk

1 medium free-range egg, beaten

FOR THE BUTTERSCOTCH SAUCE

75g/2³⁄₄ oz light muscovado sugar

50g/1³⁄₄ oz butter

150ml/5 fl oz double cream

dash of vanilla extract

I use mugs to measure the ingredients instead of cups: it makes a bigger pudding! Use a regular 300ml/10 fl oz coffee mug to measure.

Empty the first 6 mugfuls into a bowl with the spices; then add the milk and egg. Pour the mixture into a buttered 1 litre/1³⁄₄ pint pudding bowl. Cover with a double layer of buttered foil, making a pleat in the centre to allow for the contents to rise. Tie the foil securely with string, then place in a steamer or large saucepan containing enough water to come halfway up the sides of the bowl. Check the water level during the cooking, topping up with boiling water if necessary. Steam for about 2¹⁄₂ hours.

Make the butterscotch sauce by placing everything in a saucepan and heating it gently until the sugar dissolves. Boil for 3 minutes, stirring, then decant into a warmed bowl.

Turn out the pudding, and serve with the hot butterscotch sauce. And, unlike some people who might eat it with some custard or a little cream, I would inundate it with custard *and* cream – oh, and why not a scoop of ice cream, too.

Useful addresses

SCOTLAND'S TOURIST BOARD
Visit Scotland
Thistle House
Beechwood Park North
Inverness 1V2 3ED
Tel   08705 511 511
www.visitscotland.com

ARBROATH SMOKIES
R. R. Spink and Sons
Sir Williaim Smith Rd
Kirkton Industrial Estate
Arbroath DD11 3RD
Tel 01241 872023

ASPARAGUS AND SEA KALE
A.H & H.A Pattullo
Eassie Farm
by Glamis
Tayside DD8 1SG
Tel 01307 840303

AYRSHIRE BACON
Ramsay of Carluke
22 Mount Stewart Street
Carluke ML8 5ED
Tel 01555 772277
www.ramsayofcarluke.co.uk

BEEF
Donald Russell
Harlaw Road
Inverurie
Aberdeenshire AB51 4FR
Tel 01467 629666
www.donaldrusselldirect.com

BREAD, OLIVE OIL, HERBS AND MUCH MORE
Valvona & Crolla Ltd
19 Elm Row
Edinburgh EH7
Tel 0131 556 6066
www.valvonacrolla.com

BUTTERIES AND SAIR HEIDIES
The Seafield Bakery
11 Seafield Street
Cullen AB56 4SG
Tel 01542 840512

CERAMICS
Anta (head office)
Fearn
Tain
Ross-shire IV20 1XW
Tel 01862 832477

Anta (showroom)
32 High Street
Royal Mile
Edinburgh EH1 1TB
Tel 0131 557 8300
www.anta.co.uk

CLOTTED CREAM
Garden Cottage Farm
Stichill
Kelso
Roxburghshire TD5 7TL
Tel 01573 470263

FORFAR BRIDIES
McLaren Bakers
Market Street
Forfar
Tel 01307 463315

GAME
George Bower Butcher
75 Raeburn Place
Edinburgh EH4
Tel 0131 332 3469

HAGGIS, WHITE AND BLACK PUDDING
Macsween of Edinburgh
Bilston Glen
Loanhead EH20 9LZ
Tel 0131 440 2555
www.macsween.co.uk

HERBS
Scotherbs
Kingswell
Longforgan
near Dundee DD2 5HJ
Tel 01382 360642
www.scotherbs.com

HIGHLAND LAMB
North Highland Fine Lamb
Midfearn
Ardgay
Sutherland 1V24 3DL
Tel 01863 766505
www.finelamb.co.uk

LAMB, BEEF, SAUSAGES, LINDA DICK CHICKENS, DUCK EGGS
Crombie's of Edinburgh
97 Broughton Street
Edinburgh EH1 3RZ
Tel 0131 557 0111
www.sausages.co.uk

LORNE SAUSAGE, BEEF,
LAMB, SCOTCH PIES
Robertson's the Butcher
234 Brook Street
Broughty Ferry
Tel 01382 739277
www.robertsons-butchers.co.uk

OATCAKES AND PUGGY BUNS
Adamson's Bakery
Pittenweem
Fife
Tel 01333 311336

OATMEAL
Oatmeal of Alford
Montgarrie Mill
Alford
Aberdeenshire AB33 8AP
Tel 01975 562209

Aberfeldy Water Mill
Mill Street
Aberfeldy
Perthshire PH15 2BG
Tel 01887 820803

OYSTERS
Loch Fyne Smokehouse
Ardkinglas
Argyll
Tel 01499 600217
www.loch-fyne.com

SCOTCH PIES AND
SAUSAGES
Stuart's of Buckhaven
19 Randolph Street
Buckhaven
Fife KY8 1AT
Tel 01592 713413

SCOTTISH FARMHOUSE
CHEESE
Iain Mellis Cheesemonger
30a Victoria Street
Edinburgh EH1 2JW
Tel 0131 226 6215

492 Great Western Road
Glasgow G12 8EW
Tel 0141 339 3998

SELKIRK BANNOCK
Alex Dalgetty & Sons
21 Island Street
Galashiels TD1 1NZ
Tel 01896 752508
www.alex-dalgetty.co.uk

Jenners Ltd
Princes Street
Edinburgh EH2
Tel 0131 225 2442

Goodfellow & Steven Bakers
81 Gray Street
Broughty Ferry DD5 2BQ
Tel 01382 730181

SHORTBREAD
Shortbread House of Edinburgh
14 Broompark
Edinburgh EH5 1RS
Tel 0131 552 0381

SMOKED AND FRESH FISH
AND SHELLFISH
George Armstrong
80 Raeburn Place
Edinburgh EH4
Tel 0131 315 2033

SMOKED TROUT
Belhaven Trout Company
West Barns
Dunbar
Tel 01368 863244

SOFT FRUITS
G & G Sinclair
West Craigie Farm
South Queensferry EH30 9TR
Tel 0131 319 1048
www.thejamkitchen.com

STORNOWAY BLACK
PUDDING AND HEBRIDEAN
LAMB AND GAME
Charles Macleod Butcher
Ropewood Park
Stornoway HS1 2LB
Tel 01851 702445
www.charlesmacleod.co.uk

(FARMED) VENISON
Fletchers Fine Foods
Reediehill Farm
Auchtermuchty KY14 7HS
Tel 01337 828369
www.fletcherscotland.co.uk

Index

Page numbers in *italic* refer to illustrations

Acknowledgements

All props for food photography supplied by Anta and Habitat.

Thanks to the following people for helping to make it happen:

David Gordon Adams, Brechin, Angus
Kenny Adamson, baker, Pittenweem
Anne and Jo Atkinson, The Blacksmith's Coffee
   Shop, Belsay, Northumberland
Hans Baumann, Blaimore House near Huntly,
   Aberdeenshire
Margaret Benson, Edinburgh
Fiona Bird, Kirriemuir, Angus
Gavin Borthwick and his staff at George Armstrong,
   fishmonger, Edinburgh
Stewart Cameron, Executive Chef, Turnberry Hotel,
   Ayrshire
The Contini family, Valvona & Crolla, Edinburgh
Sandy and Jonathan Crombie at Crombie's the
   butcher, Edinburgh
Linda Dick, Hamildean Farm, Peebles
Clarissa Dickson Wright, Edinburgh
Humphrey Errington, Carnwath, Strathclyde
Nichola Fletcher, Fletchers Fine Foods,
   Auchtermuchty
Margaret Horn, The But 'n Ben, Auchmithie
Brenda Leddy, Stichill Farm, Kelso
Iain Macleod of Charles Macleod, butcher,
   Stornoway, Isle of Lewis

The Macsween family, haggis makers, Edinburgh
Bill McLaren, James McLaren & Son, bakers, Forfar
Alan McPherson, The Seafield Bakery, Cullen
Iain Mellis, cheesemonger, Edinburgh and Glasgow
Ritva Miettunen and Annelli Blumenthal, Finland
Heather and Sandy Pattullo, Eassie Farm,
   near Glamis
Alastair Pearson, The Old Inn, Gairloch,
   Wester Ross
John and Andrew Ramsay, Ramsay of Carluke,
   Lanarkshire
The Sinclair family at West Craigie fruit farm
   near Edinburgh
Michael Wiggans, North Highland Fine Lamb
Carol Wilson, Heswall, The Wirral
Robert Wilson of Scotherbs, Perthshire

And also, many thanks to Justin Scobie, Maxine Clark and Isobel Gillan for their brilliant work producing the book; to Jenny Dereham and Kate Truman for assiduous editing, and to Jo Roberts-Miller and Heather Holden-Brown at Headline for their patience and commitment.

Special thanks to my agent Mary Pachnos for all her hard work over the years. And, as ever, to my mother and father, Anna and Bob, my uncle Frank and Aunts Mue and Bette.

And, finally, to my husband Pat and children Euan, Faith and Jessica – thanks for eating for Scotland.

Photographic Locations

Hearty Breakfasts – *Affric River*; A Fly Cup – *Edinburgh from Carlton Hill*;
You'll Have Had Your Tea? – *Crail Harbour*; Soup on the Hills – *Cullins on Skye*;
A Lochside Picnic – *Loch Earn*; A Beach Bonfire – *West Coast*;
Hogmanay – *Dewars Distillery*; Ne'er Day – *Glenn Affric*; To a Haggis – *Callanish on Lewis*;
Chitterin' Food – *Eilean Donan Castle*